W9-BNT-563

HeRBAL SOuPs, SaLADs, BReADs & SWeeTs

HERBAL SOUPS, SALADS, BREADS & SWEETS

A Fresh from the Garden Cookbook

RUTH BASS

ILLUSTRATED BY MARY RICH

STOREY
BOOKS

Schoolhouse Road
Pownal, Vermont 05261

*The mission of Storey Communications is to serve our customers
by publishing practical information that encourages personal independence
in harmony with the environment.*

Edited by Pamela Lappies and Jeanée Ledoux
Cover and text design by Meredith Maker
Cover and interior illustrations by Mary Rich
Text production by Susan Bernier
Indexed by Nan Badgett, Word•a•bil•i•ty

Storey books are available for special premium and promotional uses and for customized editions. For further information, please call Storey's Custom Publishing Department at 800-793-9396.

Printed in The United States by R. R. Donnelley
10 9 8 7 6 5 4 3 2 1

Library of Congress
Cataloging-in-Publication Data

Bass, Ruth, 1934-
    Herbal soups, salads, breads & sweets: a fresh from the garden cookbook / by Ruth Bass; illustrated by Mary Rich.
        p. cm.
    Includes index.
    ISBN 1-58017-289-X
    1. Cookery (Herbs)   I. Title.
TX819.H4 B386 2000
641.6'57-dc21   00-029142

Contents

Herbs and soups are perfect year-round companions. On cold winter nights, add dill and parsley to warm, comforting soups such as Creamy Potato. And when you need cool refreshment on steamy summer days, try mint-topped Chilled Strawberry Soup or other cold soups.

Herbs love to accompany greens and other produce in the salad bowl as well as the garden. Try unusual combinations, such as Stuffed Nasturtiums with basil, or reinvent old standbys, such as garlicky Crisp Apple Salad with Cheese. Make savory herbal dressings, too.

Herbs are right at home in crusty loaves that take all day to make as well as quickbreads with 5-minute prep times. Throw some thyme, rosemary, and other herbs into grandma's Sausage Bread or mince a little oregano into the mix for a special Zucchini Cornbread.

Mint, sage, tarragon, lemon balm, and other herbs make surprisingly tasty additions to sweets. Try a cool herbal treat, such as Lavender Ice Cream, or sink your fork into Peppermint Angel Food Cake, a new variation of a classic dessert.

Introduction

To heal, to flavor, to beautify, to decorate — herbs have have been used in a number of important ways throughout history. The ancient Chinese and the Greeks developed medicinal drugs from herbs; the Romans exploited the culinary properties of these fragrant plants; and in medieval monasteries, the herb garden near the kitchen was a source for both food and well-being. In the 16th and 17th centuries, people became aware that a container of dried herbs and rose petals can help banish some of the unpleasant smells of daily living. Potpourris became commonplace, sachets were made to freshen clothing and storage areas, and sweet waters made from lavender and roses were sprinkled about homes.

Today, herbs are indispensable to many parts of our lives, but especially when it comes to cooking. In soups and salads, herbs are ubiquitous. With chicken, beef, and pork, they make an impact. Herbs have entered the bread world with subtlety, and they adorn many vegetables. Their use in sweets is less common, although Victorian cooks often used herbs to flavor sweet dishes, and medieval cooks did not limit use of herbs to particular courses at a feast. This volume is meant to encourage cooks to give herbs a home in all parts of meals — marry fresh or dried herbs to your appetizers, main courses, even drinks and desserts.

The best incentive for using herbs comes from having them at hand. As one contemporary chef said, "When the herbs are growing outside the kitchen door, you start using them." If you have tarragon, borage, lemon thyme, and rosemary at your fingertips, you'll reach for them and experiment. Just as you substitute a fruit or vegetable in a recipe because it's ripe, it looks good, or it's on sale, you'll find yourself snipping oregano instead of basil, cilantro instead of parsley, savory instead of marjoram.

Herb gardens in books frequently look as if they began with a landscape architect and continued with a professional gardener — someone who comes daily to pull weeds, sweep miniature stone pathways, and dust the leaves of the basil and Italian parsley. But ordinary people have herb gardens, too, or patches of herbs among the tomatoes, beans, and zucchini. Many herbs are easy to grow and require little maintenance.

Basil, any kind of parsley, dill, chervil, and garlic are easy to add to the vegetable garden. Borage, lavender, savory, rosemary, oregano, chives — all perennials — can be added to a flower garden or tucked into the crevices of a rock garden. Chives reappear so early that they are a cook's harbinger of spring. And the blossoms of oregano, lavender, chives, and borage are not only good for garnishes but also add appeal to a landscape.

For those who have no garden space, containers on the deck or patio are suitable for herbs, provided that the need for water and sun is met. A ceramic strawberry jar is a perfect place to plant small herbs such as creeping thyme or rosemary or even parsley and chives, since those will get a haircut pretty often.

Cooks in areas where frost comes late in spring and early in fall will reap a better harvest by starting with greenhouse-grown plants rather than seeds. When purchasing herbs from a nursery, be sure to ask if they've been sprayed so you'll know whether or not they need scrubbing.

For year-round access to fresh ingredients, try growing herbs indoors. One of the best and most decorative ways to do this is to plant an herb dish garden. Houseplant expert Shirl Fowler of Lenox, Massachusetts, writes that an 18-inch shallow clay bowl, perforated for drainage and set on a large plate or tray, will hold a variety of herbs, providing both a good source of flavors and a conversation piece. Embed some rocks in the potting mix to create a landscape and treat the whole thing like a terrarium. If it will be viewed from all sides, plant tall herbs in the middle, shorter ones around them, and creeping ones around the edges.

To dry your herbs, pick sprigs before they blossom, tie a bunch together, and hang the bunch upside down in a well-ventilated area. If you put the bundles inside a paper bag, you'll conquer the dust problem. When the herbs are dry, remove the stems — either shake the bag or run your thumb and forefinger along each stem. Pour the herbs into glass jars with tight covers, label them, and store them away from sunlight. Occasionally clean out the herb shelves the same way you clean out the medicine cabinet. Old herbs are as ineffective as old pills.

As an alternative to storing herbs in a cabinet, consider making a dried herbal wreath. The various herbs' shapes and aromas will make a pleasing addition to your kitchen, and having your herbs right before your eyes will inspire you while you cook. Gather sprigs into bunches and wire them onto a purchased or handmade wreath frame. (Clothes-hanger wire works fine.) Overlap the bunches so that the wire and frame are hidden. It's best not to hang the wreath directly over the stove or sink, since the moisture in these areas can cause the herbs to mold.

When substituting dried herbs for fresh herbs in a recipe, use half the recommended amount. Remember that even dried herbs that appear quite shriveled and innocuous still pack a much more powerful punch than fresh pickings do. Sometimes cutting the amount to one-third is even better.

In recent years, supermarkets have become savvy about herbs. Where once the tired parsley drooped alone, a grand variety of appealing, fresh herbs are now available. Rosemary, sage, lemon balm, mint, and other herbs cozy up to the broccoli and green beans. They are sold in large bunches or in plastic envelopes that give you a small quantity, suitable for a single meal. Grocers also sometimes sell fresh herbs in combination for a particular use, such as poultry seasoning packs. Always wash store-bought herbs. If you're going to mince them, squeeze out the excess water with a paper towel. It's difficult to chop wet herbs finely.

If you grow or purchase more fresh herbs than you can use at a given time, make herb pastes and freeze them for later. First, coarsely chop the herbs in a food processor. (Unless you are sure you want a given combination, process each herb separately. You can always combine a lump of basil and a lump of parsley later.) While the motor is still running, add enough olive oil to form a paste. Drop tablespoonfuls of the herb paste onto a cookie sheet lined with waxed paper and place it in the freezer. When the mounds are solid, put them in plastic bags, seal, and store in the freezer. An ice cube tray can also be used if it's the easy-release type.

Herbed Spinach Soup

Green and good, this soup has the bite of sorrel and fresh scallions. Its thickness comes from the potatoes.

> 4 tablespoons butter
> 8 ounces fresh spinach, finely chopped (about 1 cup)
> 4 ounces fresh sorrel, chopped (about ½ cup)
> 1 small head lettuce, shredded
> 3 scallions, white part only, shredded
> 4 medium potatoes, chopped
> 2 quarts boiling water
> 1 tablespoon chopped fresh chervil
> Salt and freshly ground pepper

1. In a large soup pot, melt the butter and add the spinach, sorrel, lettuce, and scallions. Simmer for 15 minutes, stirring occasionally.
2. Add the potatoes and boiling water to the pot. Simmer, covered, for 45 minutes.
3. Remove the potatoes, mash them, and return them to the pot, along with the chervil. Simmer for 5 minutes. Add salt and pepper to taste before serving. Do not freeze.

Cream of Asparagus Soup

When the first asparagus shoots, shaped like rosy pencils, push their way through the soil in spring, it ought to be a holiday. Once the appetite for piles of steamed stalks with butter and black pepper has been appeased, it's time for soup.

8–10 *asparagus spears, steamed gently until soft*
1 *onion, thinly sliced*
1 *cup asparagus water, reserved from the cooking*
1½ *cups water*
2 *tablespoons butter*
2 *tablespoons flour*
2 *tablespoons minced fresh parsley*
Salt and freshly ground pepper
1 *cup milk or light cream, warmed*
1 *teaspoon capers*

1. After steaming the asparagus, cut off the tips and set aside. Combine the asparagus stalks, onion, asparagus water, and plain water in a soup pot and boil for about 5 minutes.
2. Place the mixture in a blender or food processor and purée.

3. Melt the butter. Add the flour and stir until blended. Blend in the parsley and then whisk in the soup purée. Cook about 5 minutes, stirring.

4. Add salt and pepper to taste, and the warm milk or cream. Put the reserved asparagus tips in soup cups and pour the hot soup over them. Garnish with capers.

4 SERVINGS

3

Marjoram will attract bees to the garden.

Watercress Soup

Watercress — as cool as the chilly waters where it likes to grow — has a nice bite to it. The potatoes add body to this creamy soup.

3–4 *potatoes, peeled and cubed (about 2 cups)*
  2 *bunches watercress, washed carefully and finely chopped*
  2 *large white onions, cut into chunks*
  6 *cups water, slightly salted*
  2 *egg yolks*
  ½ *cup milk or light cream*
  ¼ *cup dry white wine*
   Salt and freshly ground pepper
  2 *garlic cloves, sliced in half*
  2 *tablespoons minced fresh marjoram*

1. In a large saucepan, combine the potatoes, watercress, and onions. Cover with the water. Simmer for 30 to 45 minutes over medium heat, or until the potatoes are soft.
2. Put the mixture in a food processor and purée. Return the mixture to the soup pot and heat almost to the boiling point.
3. Beat the egg yolks and milk or light cream until smooth. Stir into the soup. Add the wine, and season with salt and pepper to taste.
4. Rub soup bowls with garlic before adding soup. Garnish with the marjoram.

6 SERVINGS

Garlic Soup

It's a bit of trouble to make this soup — roasting the garlic separately and then popping it out of its peel and into the soup — but the result is a wonderfully garlicky potion.

5 heads of garlic (3 unseparated; 2 separated into
  cloves and peeled)
4 tablespoons extra virgin olive oil
½ teaspoon salt
Freshly ground pepper
2 sweet white onions, peeled and chopped
¾ pound shallots, peeled and chopped
1 pound potatoes, peeled and coarsely diced
4 cups chicken broth
1 cup light cream
1 tablespoon chopped fresh thyme
2 tablespoons chopped fresh Italian parsley

1. In a small casserole, toss the unseparated garlic heads in half the oil with the salt and the pepper to taste. Cover and bake at 350°F for 35 minutes, or until the garlic is soft when pricked with a toothpick. Set aside to cool.

2. Heat the remaining oil in a soup pot, and cook the onions slowly until soft and golden. Add the peeled garlic and the shallots; cook another 10 minutes. Add the potatoes, broth, cream, thyme, and parsley. Simmer about 25 minutes.

3. Cut the roasted garlic heads in half and squeeze out the garlic cloves from the skins. Purée the roasted garlic in a blender and add to the soup. Cook another 10 minutes and season with additional salt and pepper to taste.

4. If the soup is too thick, add more chicken broth or a little skim milk. Reheat gently before serving.

6 SERVINGS

Hot and Sour Soup

The variety of ingredients, some unfamiliar, in this soup prompted one guest to fish each one out individually and demand identification. The blending of textures and flavors, with the added bite of fresh cilantro, is extraordinary.

PORK MARINADE
- 1 teaspoon soy sauce
- 1 teaspoon white wine
- 3 teaspoons cornstarch
- 2 teaspoons sesame oil

SOUP INGREDIENTS
- ¼ pound pork, boneless
- 1 tablespoon Chinese tree ears
- 16 tiger lily buds
- 5 medium-size shiitake mushrooms
- 2 tablespoons tofu
- 2 tablespoons cornstarch
- 3 tablespoons cold water
- 1 egg
- 1 teaspoon sesame oil
- 1½ tablespoons soy sauce
- 2 tablespoons red wine vinegar
- Freshly ground pepper
- 1 teaspoon hot chili oil
- 4 cups chicken broth
- 2 teaspoons minced fresh cilantro

1. Cut the pork into ¼-inch slices. Stack the slices and shred them. Place the pork in a bowl and marinate with the soy sauce, white wine, cornstarch, and oil. Refrigerate.
2. Soak the tree ears and tiger lily buds in separate bowls of warm water until expanded and soft.
3. Rinse the tree ears and tiger lily buds. Remove the tough stems of the tree ears and the knobby ends of the lily buds. Shred both in the same manner as the pork. Thinly slice the shiitake mushrooms and cut into 1-inch lengths.
4. Cut the tofu into 2-inch pieces, ¼ inch thick.
5. Dissolve the cornstarch in a small bowl with the cold water. Beat the egg with the sesame oil in a separate bowl.
6. Combine the soy sauce, red wine vinegar, black pepper to taste, and hot chili oil and place in a serving bowl.
7. In a large soup pot, bring the broth to a boil. Add the shiitake mushrooms and tiger lily buds. Reduce the heat and simmer about 5 minutes. Add the pork, bring to a boil, and add the tree ears and tofu. Reduce the heat again and simmer 5 minutes.
8. Stir the cornstarch mixture and add to the soup slowly, stirring constantly. Pour the beaten egg in wide circles over the surface of the soup, breaking up the resulting ribbons with a spoon.
9. Pour the hot soup into the serving bowl containing the soy sauce mixture and sprinkle the cilantro over the top.

6–8 SERVINGS

Creamy Potato Soup

Sometimes potatoes are just an aside in a soup. In this case, they take center stage and play the part perfectly.

3   *pounds potatoes*
2   *quarts water*
1   *teaspoon salt*
1   *large sweet onion, chopped*
1½ *tablespoons finely snipped*
      fresh dill

2   *teaspoons freshly ground pepper*
2   *tablespoons butter*
1   *cup plain yogurt*
¼   *cup chopped fresh Italian parsley*
      or cilantro for garnish

1. Wash and peel the potatoes and cut into cubes. In a large pot, cover them with salted water and bring them to a boil. Reduce the heat and simmer for 10 minutes.
2. Add the onion and simmer for another 10 minutes or until the potatoes start to fall apart. Add the dill, pepper, butter, and yogurt, one at a time, stirring each into the soup. Bring back to a simmer and serve, garnished with parsley or, for a spikier taste, a bit of cilantro. If the soup is too thick, add a little warm milk.

4 SERVINGS

Soup

a canned one is distant,

and freshly pressed garlic

with a fresh taste.

for 5 minutes without

epper to taste. Simmer

to the soup. Heat

thickened.

Chili Pepper Soup

Some soup is hot to the touch. Some soup is even hotter to the palate. This one is both. It's for the adventurous, not those who prefer a clear broth with a little rice. Keep in mind that a habanero pepper is 1,000 times hotter than a jalapeño, and choose accordingly.

4–8 *dried chili peppers*
2 *quarts milk*
Large sprig of fresh rosemary
2 *tablespoons whole coriander seeds*
2 *bay leaves*
1 *jalapeño or habanero pepper, seeded*
4 *tablespoons butter*
2 *sweet white onions, coarsely chopped*
1 *teaspoon salt*
4 *large garlic cloves, minced*
2 *teaspoons ground cumin*
8 *cups corn kernels, fresh if possible (otherwise,*
   dry-pack canned)
Chives for garnish, finely snipped

1. Soak the dried chili peppers in warm water for 2 hours. Drain them, pat dry, split, remove the seeds, and chop.
2. In a saucepan, combine the milk, rosemary, coriander seeds, bay leaves, and hot pepper. Cook over low heat until it is just starting to simmer. Remove from heat and let stand, covered, for 15 minutes.
3. Melt the butter in a large pot over medium heat. Add the onions and salt and cook gently until golden. Add the garlic and cumin. Cook, stirring, until the cumin gives off its aroma.
4. Stir in the corn and chopped chili peppers and cook over low heat for another 5 minutes.
5. Strain the herb-flavored milk into the corn mixture and simmer for about 15 minutes. Purée about a third of the soup in a blender and return it to the pot.
6. Taste and correct the seasonings. Serve hot, garnished with a sprinkle of chives.

8 SERVINGS

Fish Chowder

Asked what kind of fish was in her delicious chowder, a Nova Scotia fisherman's wife answered that she just went to the freezer and took out whatever was available. The fish chunks were all very white, and the broth was white and sweet, something like this filling soup.

1½ pounds white fish fillets
2 cups water
3 medium potatoes
2 scallions
¼ cup diced salt pork
1 onion, chopped
1 teaspoon chopped fresh thyme
½ cup chopped fresh parsley
3 cups milk
1 tablespoon chopped fresh tarragon
Salt and freshly ground pepper

1. Cut the fish into chunks and put it in a pot with the water. Simmer over medium heat for 3 or 4 minutes. Remove the pot from the burner and set aside.
2. Peel the potatoes and cut into paper-thin slices. Cut the scallions into 1-inch pieces and shred.

3. In a large soup pot, cook the salt pork until it is golden brown. Remove the browned pieces with a slotted spoon and place on a double thickness of paper towels to drain.
4. Drain from the pot all but 2 tablespoons of the pork fat. Add the chopped onion, the thyme, and half the parsley. Cook for 2 or 3 minutes until softened. Pour the fish cooking liquid into the pot. Add the potatoes, scallions, salt pork, and enough water to cover. Boil until the potatoes are cooked, about 10 minutes.
5. Add the fish, milk, tarragon, and salt and pepper to taste. Heat thoroughly, but don't boil. Ladle the soup into bowls and sprinkle the remaining parsley over the top of each serving.

4–5 SERVINGS

Pat's Tomato Soup

Thick, hot, and hearty, this soup cries for thick slices of Italian bread —
then it's a supper all by itself. It was developed by Pat's mother-in-law, a
farmer's wife, and makes a potful, so leftovers may be frozen for another day.

SOUP INGREDIENTS
- *1 peck ripe tomatoes (8 quarts)*
- *3 onions*
- *½ bunch celery*
- *7 sprigs fresh parsley*
- *7 whole cloves*
- *6 bay leaves*
- *2 sprigs fresh basil*

PASTE INGREDIENTS
- *¾ cup flour*
- *½ cup sugar*
- *2 tablespoons salt*
- *½ teaspoon freshly ground pepper*
- *½ pound butter*

1. Wash the tomatoes, cut into quarters, and chop for 15 seconds in a food processor. In a large soup pot, combine the tomatoes with the onions, celery, parsley, cloves, bay leaves, and basil. Stew for about 2 hours. Put through a food mill or purée in a blender.
2. To make the paste, combine the flour, sugar, salt, pepper, and butter. Add to the tomato mixture and cook until boiling.

5½ QUARTS

17

Corn and Tomato Soup

They ripen together in the summer, and they make good partners in soup — the South American natives corn and tomatoes. This big batch can be the main dish for supper.

> 2 cups cooked whole kernel corn
> 2 medium tomatoes, chopped
> 4 large stalks celery, chopped
> 1 quart cold water
> 2 tablespoons softened butter
> 3 tablespoons unbleached flour
> 1 cup milk
> ½ cup grated Monterey Jack cheese
> ½ cup chopped pimento
> 2 tablespoons minced fresh oregano
> Salt and freshly ground pepper

1. In a large soup pot, cover the corn, tomatoes, and celery with the cold water. Simmer, covered, for 30 minutes or until the vegetables are tender.
2. In a small saucepan, melt the butter and blend in the flour, making a roux. Gradually add the milk and cook until thickened, stirring frequently. Add the milk mixture to the soup pot and stir well.

3. Add the cheese, pimento, and oregano and stir until the cheese is melted. Add salt and pepper to taste and serve in heated bowls.

2 QUARTS

Zucchini Soup

At some stage of summer, almost every gardener wants to leave zucchinis on other people's doorsteps, ring the bell, and run. Yet the vegetable is so versatile that it can come to the table in a thousand disguises.

> 2 tablespoons butter
> 2 tablespoons extra virgin olive oil
> 1 medium zucchini, chopped and unpeeled (unless
>   skin is tough)
> Salt and freshly ground pepper
> 2 quarts chicken broth, homemade or canned
> ¼ pound spaghettini, uncooked
> 2 medium eggs
> 8 tablespoons grated fresh Romano cheese
> 2 tablespoons grated fresh Parmesan cheese
> 1½ tablespoons chopped fresh parsley
> 1 tablespoon chopped fresh basil

1. Heat the butter and oil in a soup pot, add the zucchini, and cook over medium heat for about 10 minutes. Do not brown. Season with salt and pepper to taste.
2. Add the chicken broth and simmer, covered, for 30 minutes.

3. In the meantime, cook the spaghettini according to the directions on the package until it is al dente. Drain under cool water to stop the cooking and set aside.
4. Whisk the eggs with the two cheeses and the herbs. Add the spaghettini and pour the pasta-and-egg mixture into the soup pot. As soon as the mixture even hints at a simmer, remove it from the burner and give it a whisk. Serve immediately.

6 SERVINGS

The flavors of basil and parsley blend well.

21

Tofu Soup

The Chinese often eat their soup last, and many times it's a hearty concoction. This one is simple, perfect as an appetizer or as a stand-alone for lunch.

1 tablespoon Chinese tree ears
2 pounds soft tofu
6 cups chicken broth
2 scallions, cut in 1-inch pieces and shredded
2 carrots, peeled and coarsely grated
1½ tablespoons light soy sauce
8 shiitake mushrooms, thinly sliced
Freshly ground black pepper
¼ cup sherry
¼ cup chopped fresh cilantro

1. Soak the tree ears in a bowl of warm water until expanded and soft, about 25 minutes.
2. Slice the tofu and cut into cubes. Drain the tree ears and rinse. Remove the hard stems and shred.
3. Bring the broth to a boil in a saucepan, adding the scallions, carrots, soy sauce, mushrooms, tree ears, and pepper to taste. Simmer for 8 minutes, or until the mushrooms are cooked.

4. Add the tofu, sherry, and cilantro and reheat almost to a simmer. Serve immediately.

6–8 SERVINGS

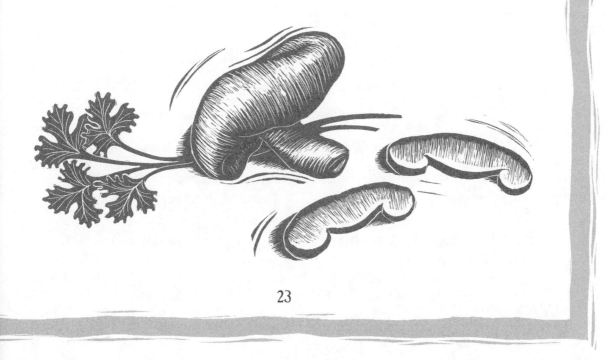

Cock-a-Leekie Soup

This country soup is older than the hills, but not the moors. It comes from Scotland and dates back to Elizabethan times. Cock-a-leekie can be a whole meal when served with a basket of hot baking-powder biscuits or cornbread. You can make it in about an hour.

2½ *pounds of boneless, skinless chicken breasts*
3 *cups water*
1 *stalk celery, diced*
2 *carrots, diced*
½ *cup barley*
1 *cup chicken broth*
2 *bay leaves*
2 *teaspoons minced fresh rosemary*
1 *teaspoon salt*
½ *teaspoon freshly ground pepper*
¾ *pound leeks, white and green parts sliced (about 1½ cups)*

1. In a large saucepan, combine the chicken breasts, water, celery, carrots, barley, chicken broth, bay leaves, rosemary, salt, and pepper. Heat to a boil. Reduce the heat, cover, and simmer for about 30 minutes.
2. Add the leeks, heat to a boil, reduce the heat again, and simmer until the chicken is tender.

3. Remove the chicken and let cool. When it is cool enough to handle, cut into bite-size pieces.
4. Skim any fat from the broth and remove the bay leaves. Put the chicken pieces back into the broth and reheat for about 5 minutes.

6 SERVINGS

French Onion Soup

You can spend a couple of hours making this soup, or you can make it in the microwave in about 15 minutes. This is the last-minute method.

> 4 *tablespoons butter*
> 1 *large sweet onion, sliced thin*
> 1 *large can beef broth (20 ounces)*
> 1 *garlic clove, minced*
> ¼ *cup dry white wine*
> *Salt and freshly ground pepper*
> 1½ *tablespoons brandy, at room temperature*
> *Melba toast rounds*
> 1 *cup shredded Swiss cheese (about ¼ pound)*

1. In a three-quart casserole, combine the butter and the separated slices of onion. Cook in the microwave for 3 minutes on high.
2. Stir in the beef broth, garlic, wine, and salt and pepper to taste. Cook in the microwave for 6 minutes on high, turning the casserole and stirring after 3 minutes.

3. Remove the casserole and immediately stir in the brandy. Divide into mugs or bowls and top with Melba toast rounds and shredded cheese.
4. Cook in the microwave for a minute on high to melt the cheese.

4–6 SERVINGS

Rosemary was an ancient remedy for headaches.

Beer and Onion Soup

People across the nation are brewing beer at home, some creating fine new versions of an age-old drink. Homebrew may be used in this recipe; otherwise use commercial stout.

3 *large white onions*
¼ *cup olive oil*
Salt and freshly ground pepper
6 *cups chicken broth*
2 *bottles dark beer*
3 *bay leaves*
1 *teaspoon minced fresh rosemary*
⅛ *teaspoon nutmeg*
Melba toast or French bread for garnish

1. Slice the onions as thin as possible. Heat the olive oil in a soup pot and add the onions and the salt and pepper to taste. Cook until onions are light brown, stirring to prevent sticking.
2. Add the chicken broth, beer, bay leaves, rosemary, and nutmeg. Bring to a boil, then reduce the heat and simmer for about 30 minutes. The onions should be soft. Correct the seasonings to taste and remove the bay leaves.
3. Garnish with a slice of Melba toast or a crust of toasted French bread.

6 SERVINGS

Apple Onion Soup

Apple soup doesn't often grace American tables, but Hungarian cooks can vouch for its virtues. This one has the sweetness of cider, the subtle aroma of fresh sage, and the heartiness provided by potatoes.

½ pound potatoes, peeled and cubed (about 1½ cups)
3 medium sweet white onions, peeled and chopped
(about 1½ cups)
4 medium apples, peeled and coarsely chopped
(about 3 cups)
2 stalks celery, chopped (about ¾ cup)
2 tablespoons minced fresh sage
2 cups chicken broth
1 cup cider
Salt and freshly ground pepper
1 tablespoon coarsely snipped fresh chives

1. In a soup pot, combine the potatoes, onions, apples, and celery.
2. Mix the sage with the chicken broth and cider and add to the pot. Bring to a boil. Reduce the heat, cover, and simmer for about 30 minutes, or until the potatoes and apples are soft.

3. Put the contents of the pot in a food processor and purée. Return to the pot and reheat. Stir frequently. Season with salt and pepper to taste. Ladle into serving bowls and sprinkle with chives.

4–6 SERVINGS

*A bunch of chives hung in a room
was once thought to ward off evil spirits.*

Amy's Butternut Squash Soup

Butternut squash are at their best in October, November, and December, when they still have September's flavor and crispness. On a cold day, take the chill off with this hearty soup.

4 *teaspoons butter*
2–3 *medium sweet onions, chopped (about 1¼ cups)*
3 *medium crisp Cortland or Spy apples,*
    chopped (about 2½ cups)
4 *cups butternut squash, peeled and cubed*
3 *cups chicken broth*
¼ *teaspoon ground coriander*
1 *tablespoon minced fresh sage*
½ *teaspoon freshly ground pepper*
1 *cup milk, at room temperature*
½ *teaspoon ground nutmeg*
½ *teaspoon ground cloves*

1. Melt the butter over medium-high heat. Add the onions and cook until golden.
2. Add the apples, squash, and broth. Bring to a boil and cover. Reduce the heat and simmer until the squash is tender, about 20 minutes.

3. Put the squash mixture, coriander, sage, and pepper in a food processor and run until smooth. Return the mixture to the pan, and stir in the milk.
4. Cook about 3 minutes to heat through. Pour into bowls and sprinkle with a mixture of nutmeg and cloves.

6 SERVINGS

33

Matzo Ball Soup

In sickness and in health, a good chicken soup helps make the world go round. And when it's time to make matzo ball soup, the broth is crucial.

MATZO BALLS

   3 *eggs, separated*
  ½ *teaspoon salt*
  ¾ *cup matzo meal*
  1 *tablespoon minced fresh parsley*
    Pinch of cinnamon

1. Beat the egg whites until they stand in soft peaks. Blend in the yolks. Add the salt, matzo meal, parsley, and cinnamon and refrigerate for at least 20 minutes. The dough will be sticky.
2. Bring a large pot of water to a boil. Form dough into 1-inch balls and drop into the boiling water. Cover, reduce to medium heat, and cook for 45 minutes. Drain.

SOUP INGREDIENTS

    4- to 5-pound chicken
    1 large onion, sliced
    4 carrots, cut in half
    3 stalks celery, cut into fourths
    2 garlic cloves
    2 tablespoons chopped fresh parsley
    2 teaspoons snipped fresh dill
    2 teaspoons salt
    Freshly ground pepper

1. In a large soup pot, cover the chicken with water. Bring to a boil, skim off foam, and add the onion, carrots, celery, garlic, parsley, dill, salt, and pepper to taste.
2. Simmer until the chicken is tender, about 2 hours. Strain the broth and reserve the chicken for another use.
3. Heat the chicken broth in a large pot, add the matzo balls, and heat to a boil. Serve immediately.

6 SERVINGS

Minestrone

It's vegetable soup the Italian way. Italy, of course, has more ways of preparing it than Rome has hills. Here's one filled with fresh vegetables and herbs, designed to tempt the nose hours before it reaches the palate.

6 tablespoons extra virgin olive oil
2 onions, finely chopped
3 tablespoons chopped fresh parsley
2 garlic cloves, crushed
1 tablespoon chopped fresh thyme
2 tablespoons tomato paste
¼ cup water
3 large tomatoes, peeled, seeded, and chopped
¼ small cabbage, shredded
2 zucchinis, diced
3 carrots, diced
1½ quarts chicken broth
Salt and freshly ground pepper
⅓ cup uncooked rice
1–1½ cups canned white or yellow beans, drained
½ cup grated Parmesan and Romano cheese
2 tablespoons minced fresh parsley

1. In a large pot, heat the olive oil and gently cook the onions, parsley, garlic, and thyme until the onions are soft. Thin the tomato paste with ¼ cup water, add to the soup pot, and cook for about 4 minutes.
2. Add the tomatoes, cabbage, zucchinis, carrots, and chicken broth. Season with salt and pepper to taste. Simmer, covered, for about an hour.
3. Bring to a boil, add the rice, and cook until the rice is done. Add the beans and reheat. Mix the grated cheeses with the parsley and sprinkle over each bowl before serving.

10–12 SERVINGS

37

Beanie Bean Soup

Ten kinds of beans can't help but be better than one. Some stores sell 10-bean packs, so you don't have to fill your cupboard with half-used packages.

¼ cup each pinto beans, black beans, lima beans,
red kidney beans, black-eyed peas, navy beans,
green split and yellow split peas, lentils, and
garbanzo beans
2 tablespoons barley
2 quarts water
1–2 pounds hot Italian or kielbasa sausage, cut into
1-inch chunks
1 bay leaf
3 garlic cloves, minced
1 can tomato purée (28 ounces)
2 hot, dried chili peppers, minced
Juice of one large lemon
1 tablespoon chopped fresh marjoram
1⅓ teaspoons chopped fresh thyme
Salt and freshly ground pepper

1. Wash the beans and the barley thoroughly. Place in a pot, cover with water, and soak overnight.
2. In the morning, drain the beans and barley. Add the water, sausage, bay leaf, and garlic. Bring to a boil over high heat. Reduce the heat and simmer for 2½ hours, stirring occasionally.
3. Add the tomato purée, chili peppers, lemon juice, marjoram, thyme, and salt and pepper to taste. Simmer an additional 30 minutes. Remove the bay leaf before serving.

8 SERVINGS

Lemony Cabbage Soup

This is a hearty dish, partly Russian in its ancestry, and it's not hard to imagine a windswept St. Petersburg landscape with men in fur hats and women in heavy scarves bending their heads to avoid the cold. You can make a meal of this on a chilly winter day.

1½ pounds lean beef, cut into 1-inch cubes
2 onions, chopped
2 bay leaves
1 tablespoon chopped fresh marjoram
2 garlic cloves
3 quarts cold water
1 medium head of green cabbage, shredded
4 medium tomatoes, chopped (2 cups)
¼ cup brown sugar
Juice of two lemons
Salt and freshly ground pepper
Plain yogurt for garnish

1. Cover the beef, onions, bay leaves, marjoram, and garlic with the water and simmer, covered, for 1½ hours.
2. Remove the bay leaves. Add the cabbage, tomatoes, sugar, lemon juice, and salt and pepper to taste. Continue to cook until the meat and cabbage are tender, about 30 minutes.
3. The meat may be removed and reserved for another use or left in the soup. Before serving, add a dollop of yogurt to each bowl.

8 SERVINGS

*Bay leaves were made into crowns to honor
ancient poets and heroes.*

41

Pea Soup

After the baked ham dinner comes the pea soup, this time flavored with fresh oregano.

½ cup dried split peas
4 cups water
1 hambone
1 medium onion, chopped
1 tablespoon minced fresh
   oregano

2 tablespoons butter
1 tablespoon flour
Salt and freshly ground pepper
1 cup milk or light cream, warmed
2 tablespoons chopped fresh
   curly parsley

1. Cover the peas with cold water and soak several hours or overnight.
2. Rinse the peas. Add the water, hambone, onion, and oregano. Simmer 3 hours or until the peas are soft.
3. Purée the soup mixture in a food processor or blender.
4. In a small pan, melt the butter and stir in the flour until smooth. Return the soup mixture to the pot and stir in the butter and flour mixture. Add salt and pepper to taste.
5. Add the milk or light cream and reheat just short of boiling. Garnish with the parsley.

6–8 SERVINGS

Lime Soup

The ingredients may sound like a gathering of misfits, but they accommodate each other nicely in a soup that lightly introduces a meal.

5 cups clear chicken broth
1 small garlic clove, peeled
2–3 tablespoons light brown sugar
¼ cup finely chopped fresh parsley
Juice of 3 medium limes (about ⅓ cup)
Salt and freshly ground pepper

1. In a medium saucepan, bring the broth to a boil. Stick a toothpick into the garlic clove (for easy removal later) and add to the broth. Add the sugar and parsley. Simmer for 10 to 15 minutes.
2. Remove from heat and stir in the lime juice. Add salt and pepper to taste. Let stand for at least an hour.
3. Remove the garlic clove. The soup may be reheated or chilled and served cold.

6–8 SERVINGS

43

Gazpacho

When in Spain, try the regional variations on this theme, especially the smooth, Andalusian version. Virtually a salad in a bowl, gazpacho quickly changed from being a stranger to being on everyone's menu in our own country. Fresh vegetables are important here.

SOUP INGREDIENTS

  3 *tomatoes, peeled*
  1 *garlic clove*
  1 *sweet white onion, cut into small chunks*
  1 *green pepper, seeded and quartered*
  1 *tablespoon chopped fresh basil*
 ⅛ *teaspoon cayenne*
 ¼ *cup white wine vinegar*
 ¼ *cup olive oil*
 ¾ *cup tomato juice*
    Freshly ground pepper

GARNISHES

  1 *cucumber, finely chopped*
  1 *small onion, finely chopped*
  1 *green pepper, finely chopped*
  1 *cup croutons*

44

1. To make the soup, liquefy the tomatoes, garlic, onion, green pepper, and basil in a blender. Add the cayenne, vinegar, olive oil, tomato juice, and pepper. Cover and chill for at least 3 hours.
2. To serve, put the garnishes — cucumber, onion, green pepper, and croutons — into chilled soup bowls and pour the very cold soup over them.

6–8 SERVINGS

Bubbie's Borscht

My mother-in-law served this soup with boiled new potatoes, which some family members would pop right into the chilled soup. That provided not only the taste sensation of hot and cold but the contrast of textures as well.

10 *large beets, peeled and grated*
Handful of beet greens, coarsely chopped
2½ *quarts water*
1 *onion, minced*
2 *garlic cloves, minced*
2½ *teaspoons salt*
2 *tablespoons sugar*
Juice of two lemons
1 *cup sour cream or plain yogurt*
Freshly ground pepper
4 *tablespoons snipped fresh chives*

1. Combine beets, greens, water, onion, garlic, and salt in a soup pot. Bring to a boil, reduce the heat, and simmer for about an hour.
2. Add the sugar and lemon juice. Cook for another 10 minutes and correct the seasoning. Chill.

3. Pour into chilled bowls, add a dollop of sour cream or yogurt, and sprinkle with pepper to taste and chives.

8 SERVINGS

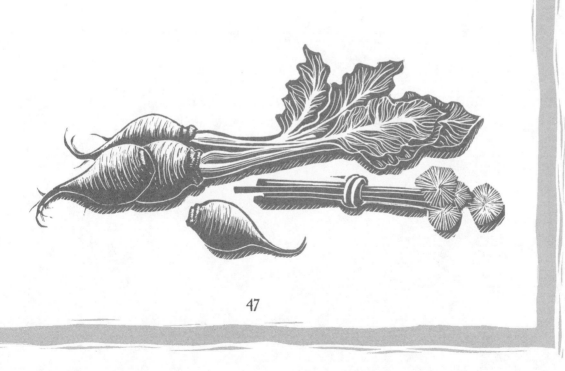

Summer Carrot Soup

When carrots are fresh from the garden and so much sweeter than in midwinter, take the time — only 20 minutes — to make this soup. Then, let it cool for a couple of hours before serving.

6–8 fresh carrots, diced (about 3 cups)
2 scallions, slivered (about ¼ cup)
1 small celery stalk, chopped
1 teaspoon snipped fresh dill
3 cups chicken broth
Salt and freshly ground pepper
½ cup plain yogurt
3 tablespoons finely snipped fresh chives

1. In a saucepan, cook the carrots, scallions, celery, and dill in the chicken broth until the vegetables are tender. Set aside to cool.
2. Purée the cooled mixture and add salt and pepper to taste.
3. Pour the soup into a covered glass or plastic container (not metal) and chill for at least 2 hours before serving.
4. To serve, top each bowl with a dollop of yogurt and sprinkle with chives.

4–6 SERVINGS

Salad Soup

Salad vegetables may look limp and unlovely after dinner, but they don't have to be thrown away. Forget the guilt trip and make soup.

> 4 *cups leftover dressed salad*
> 1 *cup buttermilk*
> 1½ *cups plain yogurt*
> ¼ *cup sour cream*
> 1 *tablespoon lemon juice*
> 2 *garlic cloves*
> 2 *tablespoons minced fresh basil*
> 6 *tablespoons water*
> *Salt and freshly ground pepper*
> 2 *medium tomatoes, diced (1 cup)*

1. Place the salad, buttermilk, yogurt, sour cream, lemon juice, garlic, basil, and water in a blender or food processor and purée until smooth. Season with salt and pepper to taste.
2. Pour into a large serving bowl and stir in the diced tomatoes. Serve chilled.

3–4 SERVINGS

Mint represents virtue.

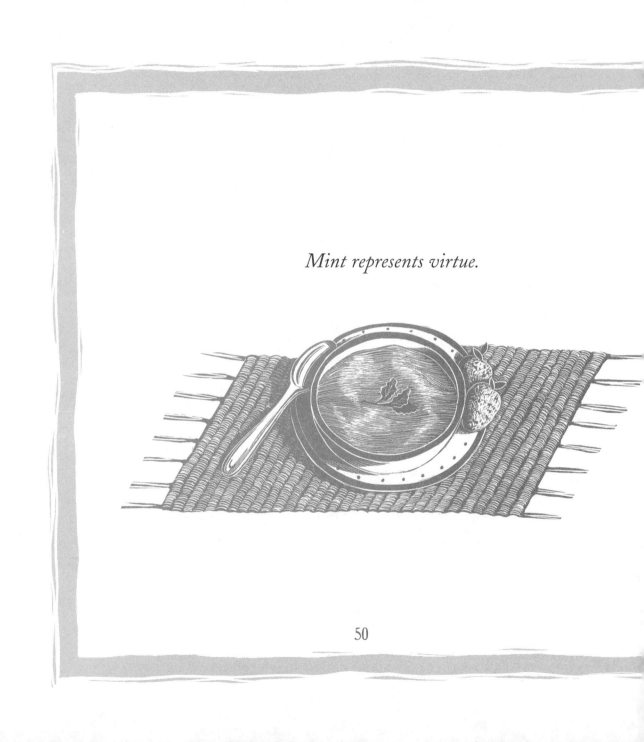

Chilled Strawberry Soup

An ice-cold fruit soup in a chilled bowl tames the heat of July. Look for strawberries that are ripe but firm. If you're picking the berries yourself, harvest them in the afternoon when they've gained sweetness from the sun.

> 1 quart fresh strawberries
> 1 cup sugar
> 1 cup plain yogurt
> 2 teaspoons minced fresh mint
> 4 cups ice water
> ¾ cup dry white wine

1. Chop the strawberries in a food processor and then force them through a sieve. Mix in the sugar, yogurt, and mint.
2. Add the ice water and white wine and sample for sweetness. Chill for at least 2 hours before serving.

8 SERVINGS

Frosty Melon Soup

For this soup, consider using glass bowls, chilled until they are frosted. Filled with pale green soup, they offer up a real cooler on a hot summer's day.

> 6 *cups water*
> 1 *carrot, peeled and halved*
> ½ *teaspoon celery seeds*
> 1 *bay leaf*
> 3 *teaspoons minced fresh lemon thyme*
> 1½-*inch piece of fresh ginger root*
> 1 *honeydew melon*
> *Salt*
> *Juice of 3 limes*
> *Slim spirals of lime peel*

1. In a large saucepan, bring the water to a boil. Add the carrot, celery seeds, bay leaf, and lemon thyme. Cover, reduce the heat, and simmer for 30 minutes.
2. Strain the broth and return to the pot. Peel and shred the ginger root. Add to the pot and simmer for 15 minutes.

3. Quarter the melon, remove seeds, and peel. Cut into chunks. Place in a food processor or blender with about 1 cup of the broth and process to a smooth purée. Stir the purée into the remaining broth. Season with salt to taste. Refrigerate, covered, for at least 3 hours.
4. Just before serving, stir in the lime juice. Serve garnished with the lime peel.

4 SERVINGS

HERBAL SALADS

Fresh Mushroom, Parsley, and Radish Salad

Raw mushrooms are a real treat — smooth textured with a woodsy taste that is like nothing else in a salad dressing. This salad adds radishes for color and sharpness.

1 garlic clove, pressed
8 large white mushrooms, thinly sliced
⅓ cup minced fresh parsley
2 tablespoons lemon juice
⅓ cup extra virgin olive oil
Pinch of chopped fresh basil leaves
Salt and freshly ground pepper
6 cups mixed salad greens: arugula, chicory,
   oak leaf lettuce, Bibb lettuce
⅓ cup finely chopped radishes

1. Place the garlic, mushrooms, parsley, lemon juice, and oil in a glass bowl and toss with the basil. Add salt and pepper to taste. Marinate at least 30 minutes.
2. Add the greens and toss. Sprinkle with the radishes and serve.

2 MAIN-DISH SERVINGS

Roasted Pepper, Garlic, and Basil Salad

Peppers turn mellow and glossy under the broiler and melt in your mouth. This salad could be a handsome appetizer or a room-temperature vegetable served with the main course.

4 green bell peppers
4 red, yellow, or orange bell peppers
4 garlic cloves, minced
1 tablespoon top quality olive oil
¼ cup red wine vinegar
A bunch of basil

1. Preheat the broiler and place the whole peppers on a broiler pan. Broil under high heat, turning frequently, for about 5 minutes or until the peppers are wrinkled. The peppers can also be cooked on an outdoor grill.
2. Wrap the peppers loosely in plastic and let them cool.
3. Remove the plastic wrap. Remove the skin from the peppers — it should come off easily. Slice the peppers in narrow strips, removing the core, stalk, and seeds. Arrange the strips on a flat serving platter.
4. Mix the garlic with the oil and vinegar. Sprinkle over the peppers.
5. Slice the basil leaves into long strips and scatter over the peppers. Marinate for an hour or so at room temperature. Do not chill.

4–6 SERVINGS

*Garlic has a more intense flavor when
grown in hotter climates.*

Sun-dried Tomatoes and Rotini

The juiciness of fresh tomatoes combines with the piquant flavor of their sun-dried cousins to create an appealing salad that can be an appetizer or part of the main course. Other pasta shapes can be tried, and buying shredded mozzarella will cut a little off the 20-minute preparation time.

> ½ cup olive oil
> 2 tablespoons red wine vinegar
> 2 garlic cloves, minced
> Salt and freshly ground pepper
> 4 medium tomatoes, chopped (about 2 cups)
> 12 sun-dried tomatoes
> 12 ounces low-fat fresh mozzarella cheese, cut
>   in ¼-inch cubes
> 4 tablespoons chopped fresh basil leaves
> 4 cups cooked rotini pasta

1. In a large bowl, combine the oil, vinegar, garlic, salt and pepper to taste, and tomatoes.
2. Add the sun-dried tomatoes, cheese, basil, and pasta.
3. Toss to blend and chill for an hour.

6–8 SERVINGS

Basil represents good wishes.

Fusilli Avocado Salad

Pop a crusty loaf of bread in the oven, put this salad together, and you have a meal that's perfect for the two-career couple. If you've forgotten to pick up any of the ingredients, substitute what you do have or leave it out. It will be good anyway.

SALAD

½ *pound fusilli pasta*
1 *head loose leaf lettuce, red or green*
1 *ripe dark-skinned avocado, peeled*
¼ *pound sharp cheddar cheese*
2 *medium tomatoes*
1 *cucumber, peeled*
1 *bunch fresh broccoli (or 10 ounces frozen), cooked*
1 *onion, chopped*
¼ *pound sliced turkey or chicken*

DRESSING

>   2   tablespoons red wine vinegar
>   2   tablespoons extra virgin olive oil
>   1   tablespoon chopped fresh basil leaves
>   1   tablespoon chopped fresh parsley
>   1   garlic clove, minced
>   ¼   teaspoon dry mustard
>   Freshly ground pepper
>   ⅛   pound crumbled blue cheese (optional)

1. Cook the pasta according to package directions. Tear the lettuce into bite-size pieces. Cube the avocado, cheese, tomatoes, and cucumber. Chop the broccoli and onion. Cut the turkey or chicken into thin strips.
2. Toss the avocado, cheese, and vegetables with the turkey or chicken and the pasta.
3. Mix together the vinegar, oil, basil, parsley, garlic, mustard, pepper to taste, and blue cheese. Pour over the salad. Toss gently.

2 MAIN-DISH SERVINGS

Tortellini Salad with Pine Nuts

Tortellini salad with the added crunch of pine nuts is perfect for the picnic basket or the patio buffet. Sweet peppers, red and green, give it color. Basil and dill give it flavor.

SALAD

- 2 *pounds fresh tortellini pasta*
- 1 *large green pepper, seeded and chopped*
- 1 *large red bell pepper, seeded and chopped*
- 2 *bunches scallions, chopped, with some green tops*
- ½ *cup pine nuts, chopped*
- ¼ *cup chopped fresh basil leaves*
- ¼ *cup snipped fresh dill*
- ¼ *cup Parmesan cheese, grated*

DRESSING

- ¼ *cup balsamic vinegar*
- 1 *garlic clove, minced*
- ¼ *teaspoon salt*
- *Freshly ground black pepper*
- ¾ *cup peanut oil*

1. In a large pot of rapidly boiling water, cook the tortellini until it is al dente. The amount of time this takes will depend on the tortellini. Drain and place in a large bowl.
2. Add the peppers, scallions, pine nuts, basil, dill, and cheese. Toss gently.
3. In a small bowl, combine the vinegar, garlic, salt, and pepper to taste. Whisk in the oil until well combined.
4. Pour the dressing over the tortellini and chill.

8 GENEROUS SERVINGS

63

Mercury claims dominion over savory.
Keep it dry by you all the year,
if you love yourself and your ease.

— *Nicholas Culpeper*

Jewel Coleslaw

Rich colors make coleslaw spectacular instead of humdrum in this simple recipe. The truly adventurous could use half red and half green sweet peppers for even more color.

1 *head purple cabbage*
1 *large white onion*
1 *large green pepper*
¾ *cup balsamic vinegar*
½ *cup corn oil*
¾ *cup sugar*
½ *teaspoon salt*
2 *teaspoons minced fresh savory*
1 *teaspoon celery seeds*

1. Using the shredding blade in a food processor, shred the cabbage, onion, and green pepper. Toss together in a glass or plain white salad bowl.
2. Bring the vinegar, oil, sugar, salt, savory, and celery seeds to a boil. Pour over the vegetables and chill well.

6–8 SERVINGS

Lemon Summer Salad

In season, when lettuce is fairly tumbling out of the bins in the produce section of the grocery store or at roadside stands, a salad can be a beautiful creation. That's Linda Morgan's intent at her Antique Orchid Herbary in Virginia, where she makes this dressing. Vary the salad ingredients according to what is in season.

DRESSING

Juice of 1 large lemon (about ¼ cup)
1½ *teaspoons grated lemon peel*
  1 *small garlic clove, crushed*
  1 *teaspoon minced fresh thyme*
  1 *teaspoon minced fresh lemon thyme*
1½ *teaspoons sugar (more, if lemon is very tart)*
  ¾ *cup oil (blend safflower, olive, and vegetable oils)*
  ½ *teaspoon salt*
Freshly ground black pepper
  ⅓ *cup finely chopped parsley*

SALAD

A variety of fresh greens, freshly washed and dried
½ *cup sorrel leaves*
1 *small cucumber, chopped*
2 *scallions, sliced in thin rings*

1. To make the dressing, put the lemon juice, lemon peel, garlic, thyme, lemon thyme, sugar, oil, salt, and pepper to taste in a jar with a tight cover. Shake until the mixture is opaque. Refrigerate for at least 2 hours so the flavors will blend.
2. Gently tear the greens and place in a bowl. Add the sorrel leaves, cucumber, and scallions.
3. About a half hour before serving, add the parsley to the dressing and shake well before dressing the salad.

4–6 SERVINGS

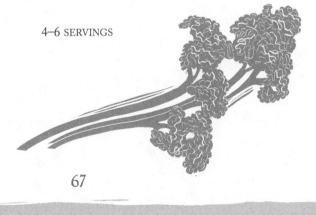

Salad Strata

One of the great things about this salad is that, unlike most of its cousins, it can be made a day ahead of time. The other great thing is that people like to eat it.

1 large head of lettuce
Several stalks of celery
2 medium green peppers
1 medium sweet onion
1 (10-ounce) package of frozen peas or sugar peas
1 cup sour cream or plain yogurt
1 cup mayonnaise, thinned with 2 tablespoons
    low-fat milk
2 tablespoons sugar
¼ pound cheddar or Monterey Jack cheese, grated
1 cup minced fresh herbs, choosing from parsley, mint,
    chervil, burnet, or lovage

1. Quarter, wash, drain, cut fine, and pat dry the lettuce. Wash and scrape the celery, and cut into small pieces. It should make about 2 cups. Wash, core, seed, and cut the peppers into strips. Slice the onion into paper-thin rings.
2. Cook the peas or sugar peas in a little salted water; rinse with cold water and drain.

3. Place the vegetables in layers in a glass bowl in the order listed, saving half of the lettuce to put on top of the other vegetables. Mix the sour cream (or yogurt) and mayonnaise together and spread over the salad. Do not stir.

4. Sprinkle the sugar over the salad and cover it with the grated cheese. Cover the bowl with plastic wrap and refrigerate for a minimum of 8 hours but preferably 24.

8 GENEROUS SERVINGS

Kate's Fresh Salsa

Jars of salsa in varying degrees of hotness line the grocery shelves and challenge the shopper to make a decision. But once you have started making your own, you won't have to decide among them anymore. There's no going back. This recipe involves only 15 minutes of preparation time. Serve it with a mound of crisp tortilla chips — they even make them nonfat now — and watch it all disappear. Or serve as a first-course salad with warm flour tortillas that can be used to scoop up the salsa.

2 large tomatoes, chopped and seeded (about 1 cup)
1 medium Vidalia or sweet onion, chopped
Juice of 1 lime (about 2 tablespoons)
⅓ cup chopped fresh cilantro
2 tablespoons chopped green chilies
2 drops Tabasco sauce
Salt and freshly ground pepper

1. Mix the tomatoes, onion, lime juice, cilantro, chilies, and Tabasco in a medium-size bowl. Add salt and pepper to taste. If you make the salsa ahead of time, leave out the chilies until just before serving.
2. Let stand for 30 minutes to blend the flavors.

2 CUPS

Cilantro, also known as coriander,
is widely used in foods throughout the world.

Cacik

Pronounced "jah-jik," cacik is a Middle Eastern specialty made with lots of yogurt and dill. To vary the recipe, add ½ teaspoon of ground cumin to the yogurt mixture or increase the dill.

2 cups plain yogurt
1 tablespoon finely snipped fresh dill or 1 teaspoon
    ground dried
2–3 large garlic cloves, chopped and crushed
1 medium cucumber, peeled and diced
3–4 parsley sprigs

1. Mix yogurt, dill, and garlic in a glass or ceramic bowl. Cover and refrigerate for at least 3 hours.
2. Gently stir in the cucumber pieces just before serving. Garnish with parsley sprigs.

6–8 SERVINGS

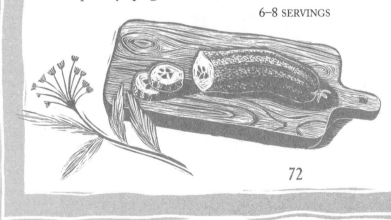

72

Herbed Vegetable Salad

For a colorful salad that you can make hours before dinnertime, try this melange of vegetables and fresh herbs.

5 cups carrots, green beans, cauliflower, and broccoli
   in any combination, cut into bite-size pieces
1 red onion, thinly sliced
½ cup salad oil
½ cup cider vinegar
2 tablespoons lemon juice
1 teaspoon each minced fresh oregano, basil,
   and rosemary
1 garlic clove, minced
½ cup minced fresh parsley

1. Cook the carrots, green beans, cauliflower, and broccoli until tender but not soft. Drain, place in a bowl, and toss gently.
2. Separate the onion slices into rings and arrange on top of the other vegetables.
3. Blend the oil, vinegar, lemon juice, oregano, basil, rosemary, garlic, and parsley and pour over the vegetables. Chill for several hours.

6–8 SERVINGS

Shrimp Dill Salad

The sweetness of raspberry vinegar, the richness of ripe avocados, and the bite of shallots, garlic, and mustard create a winning combination in this attractive summer salad.

2 tablespoons chopped shallots
6 garlic cloves, chopped (about 1 tablespoon)
1 tablespoon Dijon mustard
1 tablespoon honey
1 tablespoon raspberry vinegar
1 tablespoon red wine vinegar
½ cup snipped fresh dill
1 tablespoon chopped fresh parsley
⅔ cup peanut oil
1 pound shrimp, cooked and peeled
1 head Boston lettuce, torn
2 ripe avocados, thinly sliced
2 tomatoes, thinly sliced

1. Mix the shallots, garlic, mustard, honey, vinegars, dill, parsley, and oil. Beat until well blended and pour over the shrimp. Allow to marinate 3 to 4 hours.
2. Remove the shrimp and arrange on lettuce leaves. Garnish with avocado and tomato slices.

4 SERVINGS

Chicken Salad in a Lily

If you have unsprayed day lilies in your garden, consider serving them stuffed with this chicken salad. The day lilies are not only lovely containers but edible ones. It is best to cook the chicken a day or two before preparing this elegant party fare.

BASIC CHICKEN SALAD

3-pound whole chicken
4 quarts water
½ cup chopped fresh parsley
4 tablespoons chopped sweet onion
2 teaspoons finely chopped fresh tarragon or 1 teaspoon dried
Pinch of dried rosemary
Pinch of fresh lemon thyme, burnet, or lovage
14–15 large celery stalks
4 cups mayonnaise
12 unsprayed day lilies

OPTIONAL INGREDIENTS
   black olives
   1 Red Delicious apple, diced
   almonds, slivered
   peanuts
   mandarin oranges
   diced roasted peppers
   sliced water chestnuts

1. In a large soup pot, combine the chicken, water, parsley, onion, tarragon, rosemary, and whichever herb you are using. Chop 6 stalks of the celery and add to the pot. Cook until the chicken meat falls away from the bone, about 40 to 50 minutes. Cool.
2. Debone and skin the cooled chicken and cut into bite-size pieces until you have 4 cups. Reserve any extra chicken and the broth for another use. Mince the remaining celery. (You should have about 4 cups.)
3. Combine the chicken, celery, and mayonnaise. Add any of the optional ingredients, in any combination that suits your eye and taste buds.
4. Stuff the day lilies with the chicken salad just before serving.

12 SERVINGS

Fruited Chicken Salad

Grapes and chicken marry well. For the best results, take the time to slice the grapes in half. This dish is perfect for a summer lunch, the centerpiece of a picnic, or a cool supper.

2 *large boned chicken breasts, cooked and*
     cubed (about 4 cups)
2 *celery stalks, chopped (about ¾ cup)*
1 *(11-ounce) can mandarin oranges, drained*
1 *cup seedless white grapes, halved*
¼ *cup mayonnaise*
3 *tablespoons low-fat milk*
Juice of half a lemon
2 *tablespoons finely chopped fresh parsley*
Salt
2 *teaspoons celery seed*
2 *teaspoons finely chopped fresh savory or 1 teaspoon dried*
Bibb lettuce

1. Combine the chicken, celery, oranges, and grapes. Set aside.
2. Thin the mayonnaise with the milk and lemon juice. Add the parsley, salt to taste, celery seed, and savory. Mix well.
3. Combine the dressing with the chicken mixture and chill well. Serve cupped in leaves of Bibb lettuce.

6 SERVINGS

Greek Rice Salad

The starches — potatoes, pasta, and rice — make summer salads that can be served chilled or at room temperature for full flavor. While white rice will do, brown is recommended, not only for its nutritional value but also for its nutty taste.

1½ cups uncooked rice
2 cups water
2 tablespoons white vinegar
3½ tablespoons olive oil
1 teaspoon finely chopped fresh oregano, or
    ½ teaspoon dried
¼ cup finely chopped fresh parsley
1 garlic clove, minced or crushed
Salt and freshly ground pepper
10–12 Greek olives, green and black, pitted
    and chopped
1 head Bibb lettuce, separated, or 12 ounces fresh
    spinach leaves
½ cup crumbled feta cheese

1. Cook the rice according to the package directions but without adding any flavorings or butter.

2. While the rice cooks, mix in a jar the water, vinegar, oil, oregano, parsley, garlic, and salt and pepper to taste. Cover and shake well.
3. Combine the cooked rice and chopped olives in a glass or ceramic bowl. Pour the dressing over the mixture and toss.
4. Arrange the cuplike leaves of the Bibb lettuce or the stemmed spinach leaves on 4 salad plates. Fill with the rice and olive mixture and sprinkle the feta cheese on top.

4 SERVINGS

Tabbouleh

Throughout the Middle East, this minty salad is made with many variations. The key ingredients, however, are the bulgur (cracked wheat), parsley, and mint, and the result is a refreshing and satisfying salad. This regional version adds ½ cup cooked, cooled peas.

½ cup bulgur
2 cups boiling water
½ cup peas
3 ripe tomatoes
1 cucumber, peeled
5 scallions
4 tablespoons olive oil
Juice of one lemon
1 large bunch mint (about 8 ounces), finely chopped
1 large bunch flat-leaf parsley (about 8 ounces),
    finely chopped
Salt and freshly ground pepper

1. Put the bulgur in a large bowl and pour the boiling water over it. Cover and let stand for at least 30 minutes, until all the water is absorbed.
2. Cook the peas until tender but not soft, about 4 minutes. Drain and set aside to cool.
3. Dice the tomatoes and cucumber into small pieces. Thinly slice the scallions and add to the tomatoes. Mix the oil and lemon juice.
4. Combine the bulgur with the peas and the tomato mixture and stir gently. Add the mint, parsley, and salt and pepper to taste and toss with the oil and lemon juice. Set in a cool place for about an hour so the flavor can develop.

6–8 SERVINGS

Marinated Potato Salad

Potato salad is such a traditional favorite that nearly every family loves a particular one. The potato, a pale, bland, yet wonderful vegetable, occasionally needs new treatment. This variation is simple but tasty.

8 large potatoes, peeled
1 yellow onion, finely chopped
2 garlic cloves, minced
3 teaspoons minced fresh oregano
2 tablespoons olive oil
2 tablespoons cider vinegar
½ cup mayonnaise
Salt and freshly ground pepper
3 hard-cooked eggs
4–6 frilly lettuce leaves
Paprika and parsley sprigs for garnish

1. Cook the potatoes until tender but not soft. Cool, then cut into cubes.
2. Make a marinade by mixing the onion, garlic, and oregano with the oil and vinegar.

3. While the potatoes are still warm, pour the marinade over them and toss as gently as possible. Cover with plastic wrap and refrigerate.
4. Just before serving, mix in the mayonnaise and salt and pepper to taste. Chop the hard-cooked eggs and gently toss with the salad. Arrange on a bed of lettuce. Sprinkle paprika on top and tuck parsley sprigs around the edges for color.

4 SERVINGS

Yellow Beets and Green Bean Salad

For this dish you'll want freshly picked beans with plenty of life in them. It will take about 30 minutes to prepare this salad, including cooking the vegetables.

½ pound crisp green beans with
    the ends snipped
3 medium-size yellow beets, diced
1 teaspoon minced fresh tarragon
2 tablespoons chopped fresh parsley
5 ounces plain low-fat yogurt
1 tablespoon tahini (sesame seed paste)
1 tablespoon fresh lemon juice
1 garlic clove, crushed
Salt and freshly ground pepper

1. In a saucepan, cook the green beans in rapidly boiling water for 7 minutes or until they are tender but crisp. In a separate saucepan, cook the beets until they are tender. (You may cook both in the microwave according to your oven's instructions if you prefer.) Cool rapidly under cold running water and peel the beets.
2. Combine the beans with the beets, the tarragon, and half the parsley in a medium-size serving bowl. Mix well but gently.

3. In a small bowl, combine the yogurt, tahini, lemon juice, garlic, and salt and pepper to taste. Mix well. Stir the yogurt mixture into the green bean mixture and garnish with the remaining parsley. Serve immediately.

4 SERVINGS

Parsley is rich in vitamin C and iron.

Adriatic Bean Salad

Black beans need better publicity. They are an underrated source of nutrients and, combined with the sweet-and-sour flavor of balsamic vinegar, they taste spectacular. Colorful peppers and bright parsley give the salad visual pizazz. For a little more bite, substitute cilantro for the parsley.

1 large yellow pepper
1 large green pepper
2 cups cooked black beans (or one 16-ounce can)
2 tablespoons coarsely chopped sweet onion
1 tablespoon balsamic vinegar
1 tablespoon olive oil
1½ tablespoons water
1 teaspoon minced fresh thyme
3 garlic cloves, minced
1 teaspoon minced fresh marjoram
Salt and freshly ground pepper
½ cup chopped fresh parsley

1. Chop the peppers, removing the seeds. In a bowl, combine the peppers with the beans. The beans should be warm.
2. In a small jar with a tight-fitting lid, combine the onion, vinegar, oil, water, thyme, garlic, marjoram, and salt and pepper to taste. Shake until they are combined. Pour over the bean mixture and toss gently.
3. Sprinkle the parsley over the top, cover with plastic wrap, and chill for a minimum of 2 hours.
4. Stir in the parsley just before serving.

4 SERVINGS

Oregano means "joy of the mountain."

Three Bean Salad

For color and for speed of preparation, it's hard to beat this salad, which is a great addition to any buffet.

2 cups cooked chick peas or 1 (16-ounce) can, drained
2 cups cooked red kidney beans or 1 (16-ounce) can, drained
2 cups green beans, cooked until tender crisp or 1 (16-ounce) can, drained
1 sweet onion, peeled and sliced paper-thin
2–4 garlic cloves, minced
2 tablespoons finely chopped oregano
Salt and freshly ground pepper
⅔ cup olive oil
¼ cup vinegar

1. In a large bowl, combine the chick peas, kidney beans, green beans, and onion.
2. Mix the garlic, oregano, salt and pepper to taste, oil, and vinegar and pour over the bean mixture. Toss gently. Let stand at room temperature for at least 30 minutes. Serve warm or chilled.

8 SERVINGS

Green Bean Salad

When evenings are so warm that no one wants the stove turned on, and green beans are young and slender and crisp, prepare this recipe in the cool of the morning. The key to success here is marinating the fresh beans while they are still hot.

SALAD

3 teaspoons snipped fresh dill or an equal amount
    of chopped fresh oregano
½ cup olive oil
3 tablespoons white vinegar
1 tablespoon balsamic vinegar
1 pound fresh, young green beans
4–6 frilly lettuce leaves

SUGGESTED GARNISHES
hard-cooked egg
red bell pepper
Greek olives
tomato

1. Mix the dill or oregano, oil, and vinegars.
2. Cook the beans until tender but still firm. Drain well and immediately pour the marinade over the beans while they are still hot. Cover the bowl and refrigerate.
3. Serve on a bed of leaf lettuce. Garnish with wedges of egg white, half circles of red pepper, spicy Greek olives, and/or tomato wedges.

4 SERVINGS

Lemonnaise Green

If you want a mayo that's a little different, try this one. Serve it over tossed salads, coleslaw, or even as a dip for raw vegetables. The first half of the recipe will stand alone if you don't want to bother with the green part.

LEMONNAISE
1 egg white
½ teaspoon dry mustard
½ teaspoon sugar
⅛ teaspoon salt
1 cup canola oil
Juice of ½ lemon (about 1½ tablespoons)
½ tablespoon hot water

1. In a food processor or blender, combine the egg white, mustard, sugar, and salt. Blend until the mixture is a little frothy.
2. With the food processor still running, gradually add half the oil, pouring in a thin stream. Slowly add 1 tablespoon of the lemon juice.
3. With the processor running again, dribble in the rest of the oil and lemon juice. Add the hot water and continue to mix until thoroughly blended. The mixture can be used at once or refrigerated.

ABOUT 1 CUP

GREEN INGREDIENTS

4–6 *broccoli florets, cooked (about ¼ cup)*
⅓ *pound kale, cooked (¼ cup)*
1 *tablespoon chopped fresh parsley*
1 *tablespoon snipped fresh chives*
1 *teaspoon chopped fresh tarragon*
1 *teaspoon chopped fresh chervil*
1 *teaspoon snipped fresh dill*
¾ *cup Lemonnaise*
Salt and freshly ground pepper

1. In a food processor or blender, combine the broccoli and kale with the herbs and blend until smooth.
2. Add the Lemonnaise and the salt and pepper to taste and blend again until well mixed.
3. Place in a glass or plastic container and chill for at least 2 hours before using.

Rosemary Tarragon Vinegar

Sprigs of these two herbs are visually intriguing when bottled up together — and their flavors mesh. For the best results, seek out white wine or champagne vinegar.

3 large sprigs rosemary
3 large sprigs tarragon
2 cups white wine or champagne vinegar

1. Put the herbs into a pint bottle and pour in the vinegar (or divide the ingredients between two smaller bottles). Use sterilized glass bottles.
2. Seal nonmetallic lids with hot paraffin wax. Store for 2 to 3 weeks before using.

1 PINT

96

Thyme, Lemon Peel, and Black Pepper Vinegar

With spirals of lemon peel climbing inside the bottles, this vinegar makes a pretty gift. The addition of 2 or 3 hot dried red peppers will radically change its personality.

3 *large sprigs fresh thyme*
1 *long spiral lemon peel*
2 *heaping teaspoons black peppercorns*
2 *cups white wine vinegar*

1. Put the thyme, lemon peel, and peppercorns into a pint bottle or two 8-ounce bottles. Use sterilized glass bottles. Add the wine vinegar. Seal nonmetallic lids with hot paraffin wax.
2. Store for a month or so before using, and remember to give the bottles a gentle shake every day or two to keep the peppercorns moving. You could also add the dried concoction called pickling spice to this vinegar for quite a different effect.

1 PINT

Creamy Herb Salad Dressing

With mustard, a mixture of herbs, and the tang of capers, this dressing puts zing into a salad of crisp, mixed greens. It will also go with vegetables that have been cooked for a few minutes and chilled: snow peas, for instance, or green beans or tiny florets of broccoli.

HINT: If you only occasionally use buttermilk, look for the powdered variety, which can be stored on a shelf. You will always have buttermilk at hand in any quantity.

⅔ cup sour cream or yogurt
½ cup buttermilk
2 tablespoons minced capers
2 tablespoons minced fresh parsley
2 teaspoons snipped fresh dill
2 teaspoons minced fresh basil leaves
1 garlic clove, minced
1 teaspoon dry mustard
1 tablespoon lemon juice
¼ teaspoon celery seeds
Salt and freshly ground pepper

1. Whisk together the sour cream or yogurt, buttermilk, capers, parsley, dill, basil, garlic, mustard, lemon juice, celery seeds, and salt and pepper to taste. Let stand for at least 30 minutes so the flavors will blend.
2. Combine with a salad. Preparation time is about 15 minutes.

1½ CUPS

Garlic Mayonnaise

It's not hard to make mayonnaise, and the homemade kind is quite a nice change from what comes in a commercial jar. Here's one spiked with garlic.

> 2 egg yolks
> Juice of one medium lemon (about 3 tablespoons)
> 4–5 garlic cloves, minced
> 2 teaspoons minced fresh parsley
> 1 tablespoon minced shallots
> 2 teaspoons Dijon mustard
> ¾ teaspoon salt
> Freshly ground pepper
> ½ cup extra virgin olive oil

1. In a blender or food processor, combine the egg yolks, lemon juice, garlic, parsley, shallots, mustard, salt, and pepper to taste. Blend until smooth.
2. With the blender still going, pour in the oil in a thin stream. The mayonnaise will thicken as the oil is poured in.

¾ CUP

Ensalada de Naranjas

The sweetness of navel oranges and the crispness of cucumbers put fruit and vegetables in happy combination in this traditional Mexican salad.

1 head curly endive or approximately 12 ounces
  fresh spinach
3 navel oranges, peeled and cut into thin slices
1 large cucumber, unpeeled, sliced very thin
1 tablespoon finely chopped fresh oregano
3 scallions, cut into ¼-inch pieces
¼ cup olive oil
½ cup vinegar
Freshly ground black pepper

1. Arrange the washed and drained endive or spinach in a shallow bowl.
2. Place the orange and cucumber slices in a decorative pattern over the greens. Sprinkle the oregano and scallions on top.
3. Mix the oil, vinegar, and pepper to taste and pour over the salad.

4 SERVINGS

Crisp Apple Salad with Cheese

The traditional Waldorf salad with apples, chopped walnuts, and mayonnaise has been a staple at cafeterias for decades. This apple salad has a whole new taste and will be especially good in the fall when apples have just been picked and are at their crunchy best.

BALSAMIC VINAIGRETTE
⅓ cup extra virgin olive oil
2 tablespoons balsamic vinegar
Salt and freshly ground pepper
1 garlic clove, cut in half lengthwise with green core removed

1. Combine the oil, vinegar, salt and pepper to taste, and garlic in a small jar with a lid. Shake and let stand for at least 15 minutes, or leave in the refrigerator for a day.
2. Remove the garlic and use within 2 days.

THE SALAD

   2 *Cortland apples, unpeeled, cored, and thinly sliced*
      in wedges or circles
   1 *cup diced fennel bulb*
   1 *tablespoon minced fresh parsley*
   Balsamic vinaigrette
   2 *cups torn Boston lettuce*
   2 *cups torn romaine*
   1 *cup torn red or green oak leaf lettuce*
   1 *cup torn arugula*
  ⅓ *cup crumbled blue cheese*
   Fennel leaves for garnish

1. Put the apples — Cortlands are recommended because they stay white after they are cut, but other varieties may be used if you prefer — and the fennel in a large salad bowl. Toss with the parsley and the balsamic vinaigrette.
2. Layer the various lettuces on top. Cover with plastic wrap and refrigerate. The salad may be made 2 or 3 hours ahead of time.
3. When it is time for dinner, sprinkle the crumbled cheese on top and toss lightly. Garnish with a few fennel leaves.

8 SERVINGS

Sweet cicely represents gladness.

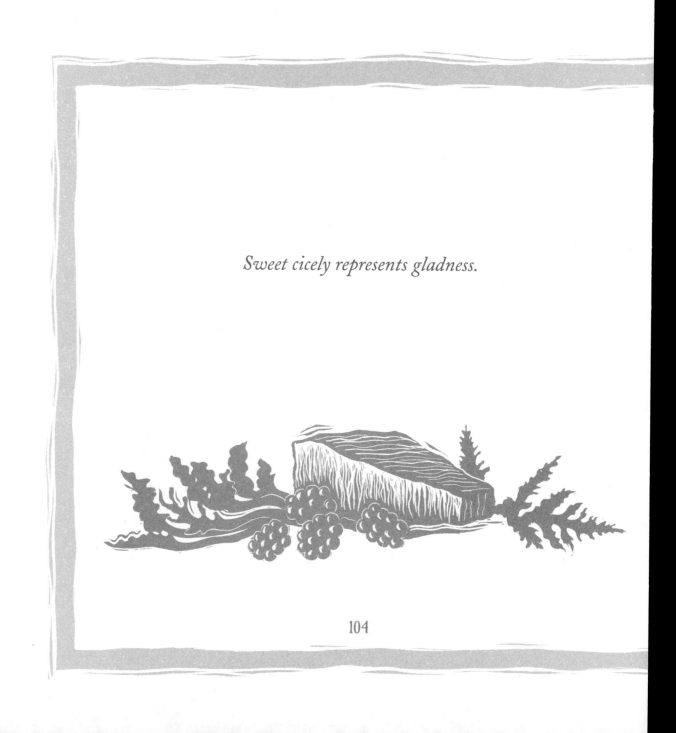

Raspberries with Chevre

A smooth-textured, well-made chevre (goat cheese) has a slight sharpness that combines well with the flavor of fresh raspberries in this pretty green, white, and red salad.

SALAD

1 head curly endive or red-leaf lettuce, freshly washed and dried
½ cup chevre
1 cup raspberries

DRESSING

1 teaspoon honey
Pinch of dry mustard
1 tablespoon white wine vinegar
3 tablespoons safflower oil
1 tablespoon sweet cicely

1. Tear the endive or red-leaf lettuce into attractive beds and cut the chevre into small pieces.
2. Arrange on a plate with the raspberries.
3. Whisk together the honey, mustard, vinegar, oil, and sweet cicely. Pour the dressing over the salad and toss gently.

4 SERVINGS

Mint Dressing for Fruit

A fruit salad is festive on a buffet table at any time of the year. Choose fruits that are in season and nicely ripened. They should be carefully washed, peeled, and sliced, then placed in a handsome bowl.

½ cup granulated sugar
1½ cups vegetable oil
Juice of 5 large lemons (about 1 cup)
1½ teaspoons salt
8-inch sprig of fresh mint leaves

1. Place the sugar, oil, lemon juice, salt, and mint in a blender. Blend until smooth.
2. Pour into a glass container, cover, and refrigerate at least 12 hours. Dribble over fruit.

3 CUPS

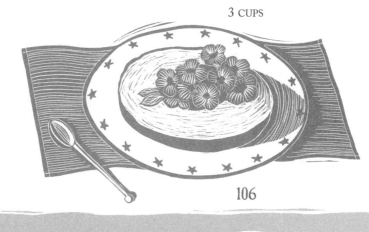

Minted Melon with Violets

A honey dressing spiked with mint makes a delicious dressing for cantaloupe. Violets add a little glamour. If they've stopped blooming, substitute pansies or Johnny-jump-ups, preferably in shades of purple.

2   *tablespoons honey*
⅔   *cup water*
1   *mint sprig*
⅔   *cup apple juice*
1   *tablespoon lemon juice*
2   *tablespoons chopped applemint*
2   *small cantaloupes*
Violets for garnish

1. Gently heat the honey in the water until it dissolves. Bring to a boil, add the mint sprig, and simmer about 10 minutes. Cool and remove the mint.
2. Combine the liquid with the apple juice and lemon juice. Add the chopped applemint.
3. Slice the cantaloupes across (not lengthwise) into 3 (1-inch) circles and remove the seeds from the center. Peel the rings. Place a ring on each salad plate and pour some of the dressing into each. Decorate with chopped and whole violets.

6 SERVINGS

Stuffed Nasturtiums

Nasturtiums not only tumble out of window boxes with a profusion of round green leaves and orange, coral pink, or yellow blossoms but also can come to the table with quite an elegant display of manners.

8 ounces cream cheese
3 tablespoons mayonnaise
¼ cup chopped nuts
1 carrot, grated (about ¼ cup)
1 tablespoon finely minced green pepper
2 teaspoons chopped fresh basil, parsley, dill, or other herb
1½ dozen brilliant nasturtium blossoms, washed
Chives for garnish

1. Soften the cream cheese with the mayonnaise. Add the other ingredients, except for the nasturtiums.
2. Roll the mixture into balls and fit into the nasturtium flowers. Top with a bit of chives or any other edible blossom.
3. Ring a platter with round, bright green nasturtium leaves and arrange the stuffed flowers in the center. These could also be served individually as an hors d'oeuvre.

6 SERVINGS

Dill was once considered a magical herb
that could ward off witchcraft.

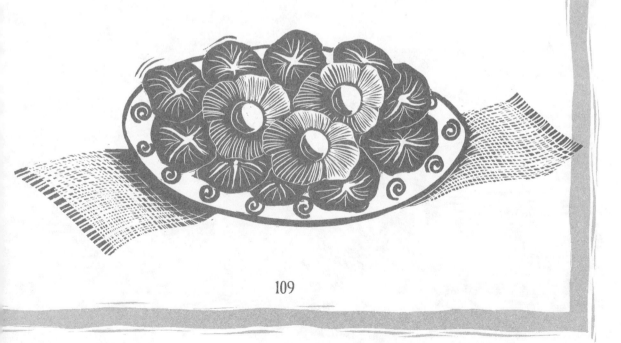

HERBAL BREADS

Thyme and Cheese Biscuits

Wheat, herbs, and cheese cause a major personality change in old-fashioned baking powder biscuits. Other herbs can be substituted for the ones here.

½ cup whole wheat flour

1½ cups unbleached all-purpose flour

3 teaspoons baking powder

1 teaspoon minced fresh thyme

½ teaspoon minced fresh parsley

½ teaspoon minced fresh rosemary

½ cup shredded Monterey Jack cheese

5 tablespoons butter

½ cup milk, possibly more

1. Preheat the oven to 450°F. Grease a cookie sheet and set aside. Mix flours, baking powder, herbs, and cheese in a large mixing bowl, using a fork. Cut in the butter. The mixture will be crumbly.

2. Add the milk and stir until the ingredients hold together. More milk may be needed.

3. Drop large spoonfuls of the sticky dough on the cookie sheet at least an inch apart. Bake 10–12 minutes or until a toothpick inserted in the center comes out clean.

1 DOZEN BISCUITS

Apple Muffins

Almost any fruit can be added to a muffin, and most of them have been —
cranberries, raisins, peaches, strawberries, blueberries. Apples are a happy
choice, too, as long as they are finely chopped.

1 *cup unbleached all-purpose flour*
½ *cup whole wheat flour*
⅓ *cup sugar*
2 *teaspoons baking powder*
½ *teaspoon salt*
¼ *cup powdered buttermilk*
½ *teaspoon nutmeg*
2 *teaspoons minced fresh sage*
4 *tablespoons butter, softened*
1 *egg*
¾ *cup water*
2 *medium apples, finely chopped (1 cup)*
½ *teaspoon cinnamon*
⅓ *cup dark brown sugar*

1. Preheat the oven to 375°F. Grease a muffin tin and set aside. In a large bowl, combine the two kinds of flour, sugar, baking powder, salt, buttermilk, nutmeg, and sage.
2. Add the butter, egg, water, and apples and mix quickly. Fill the muffin cups about two-thirds full. Mix the cinnamon and brown sugar and sprinkle on each muffin.
3. Bake for 20 minutes.

1 DOZEN MUFFINS

Sweet Potato Muffins

Sweet potatoes create a mellow, yellow muffin. This one has herbs for flavor and some zucchini for volume.

1½ cups unbleached all-purpose flour
¼ cup sugar
½ teaspoon baking powder
2 teaspoons baking soda
½ teaspoon salt
½ cup vegetable oil
½ cup brown sugar
2 eggs
1 teaspoon vanilla extract
¾ pounds sweet potatoes, cooked and mashed (1½ cups)
¾ pounds unpeeled zucchini, shredded (1½ cups)
1 tablespoon minced fresh tarragon
1½ teaspoons cinnamon

1. Preheat the oven to 375°F. Grease 2 muffin tins or line with paper muffin cups. Sift together the flour, sugar, baking powder, baking soda, and salt. In a separate large bowl, beat the oil, brown sugar, eggs, and vanilla.
2. Stir the sweet potatoes, zucchini, tarragon, and cinnamon into the oil and egg mixture. Add the flour mixture and stir until blended.
3. Pour the batter into the muffin tins. Bake for 20 minutes.

2 DOZEN REGULAR SIZE MUFFINS OR 1 DOZEN OVERSIZE MUFFINS

Aromatic Pancakes

Some brunches are breakfast. Some brunches are lunch. Pancakes with fruit and herbs create a tasty bridge between the two and are a perfect brunch offering. The adventurous will want to experiment with other fruits and other herbs. This combination produces a fragrant, tasty pancake. (Shortcut: Use 1 cup biscuit mix in place of flour, baking powder, and oil.)

> 1 egg
> ½ cup milk, possibly more
> 2 tablespoons oil
> 1 cup sifted pastry or unbleached all-purpose flour
> 2 teaspoons baking powder
> 3 tablespoons sugar
> 1 large, ripe peach, finely chopped
> 3 teaspoons minced fresh savory, or 1 teaspoon ground
> Maple syrup or yogurt

1. Beat the egg, then add the milk and oil. Sift the flour with the baking powder and sugar into the egg mixture and stir just enough to blend. Add the chopped peach, including juice, and the savory. The batter should be easy to pour, and more milk may be added as needed.

2. Lightly grease a griddle or electric skillet, heat, and pour the batter in ¼-cup amounts to make small pancakes. Flip when bubbles circle the pancakes, and serve with maple syrup or a dollop of yogurt.

8–10 PANCAKES

Scottish Scones

Tea in the British Isles means scones, one of the most delicious members of the bread family. Try these rich ones with a dollop of whipped cream — clotted cream is hard to come by in the United States — and some strawberry jam.

1¾ cups unbleached all-purpose flour
4 tablespoons sugar
2½ teaspoons baking powder
½ teaspoon salt
1½ teaspoons minced fresh lemon thyme
⅓ cup butter
2 eggs
½ cup raisins, chopped
4–6 tablespoons light cream

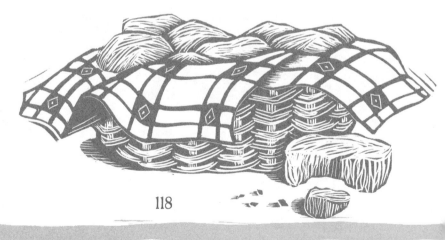

1. Preheat the oven to 400°F. Combine the flour, sugar, baking powder, salt, and lemon thyme in the bowl of a food processor. Blend in the butter until the mixture looks like fine crumbs. Do not overmix.
2. In a large bowl, beat one egg and add the flour mixture. Stir in the raisins and enough of the cream so that the dough forms a ball. Turn the dough onto a lightly floured surface and knead about 10 times. Roll out to ½-inch thickness.
3. Beat the other egg. Cut the dough into circles with a biscuit cutter (2–2½ inches), place the circles on an ungreased cookie sheet, and brush with the beaten egg. Bake for 10–12 minutes or until golden brown. Immediately remove to a wire rack to cool, or serve warm.

10–12 SCONES

*Thyme, from the Greek word for courage,
was said to invigorate warriors.*

Sausage Bread

This puts the taste of a sandwich, delicately, into a slice of crusty, flavorful bread. It's done by machine, so just prepare the ingredients, pop them into the container, and let technology take it from there.

¼ pound hot Italian sausage, casing removed
1 large shallot (all the cloves)
1 teaspoon minced fresh thyme
1 teaspoon minced fresh parsley
1 teaspoon minced fresh marjoram
1 teaspoon minced fresh rosemary
¼ cup wheat bran
2 cups unbleached all-purpose flour
½ packet active dry yeast (1½ teaspoons)
1 tablespoon sugar
1 teaspoon salt
1 tablespoon grated cheese, mixed Parmesan and Romano
¾ cup water

1. Crumble or finely chop the sausage into a nonstick pan. Peel and chop the shallot.
2. Cook the sausage, continuing to separate any lumps. After a minute or two, add the shallot and herbs. Cook until the shallot is soft but not browned, then set the mixture aside to cool.
3. Using the order prescribed by your bread machine instructions, put the meat mixture along with the bran, flour, yeast, sugar, salt, cheese, and water into the machine. Process as basic bread.

1 SMALL LOAF

NOTE: *If you don't have a bread machine, you can make this recipe by adapting the instructions for the Herbed Focaccia on page 124 or another yeast bread to fit these ingredients.*

Savory Onion Bread

The aromas of onion and garlic are mouthwatering. This bread has both, plus an assortment of other flavors that make it hard to wait for the oven to finish its work.

5 cups unbleached all-purpose flour	2 eggs
1 tablespoon sugar	3 garlic cloves, pressed
½ tablespoon salt	2 teaspoons minced sweet onion
1 packet active dry yeast	3 teaspoons minced fresh savory
(about 1 tablespoon)	1 teaspoon caraway or sesame seeds
1¼ cups milk	Freshly ground pepper
1 stick plus ⅔ stick butter, softened	½ teaspoon hot sauce

1. In a large mixing bowl, combine 2 cups of the flour with the sugar, salt, and yeast.
2. Heat the milk with the ⅔ stick butter until warm.
3. Beat the eggs and add to the flour mixture, then add the milk mixture. Beat with an electric mixer on low until the flour is moist, then increase the speed to high and beat for 2 minutes.
4. Using your hands, blend in the rest of the flour. Turn the dough out on a lightly floured surface and knead. Butter the inside of the bowl and return the dough to the bowl, turning it until the surface is entirely covered with butter. Cover and put in a warm place until the dough rises to double its original bulk.

5. In the meantime, cream the full stick of butter with the garlic, onion, savory, caraway or sesame seeds, pepper to taste, and hot sauce.

6. Punch down the dough when it is ready, remove from the bowl, and divide in half. Roll one half into an 8 x 14-inch rectangle and spread half the seasoned butter over the dough. Roll up the rectangle and pinch the edges so that it closes tightly. Tuck the ends under and place in a greased or nonstick 4 x 8-inch loaf pan. Repeat for with other half. Cover both loaves with wax paper and let rise until the dough reaches the top of the pan.

7. Place the bread in an oven preheated to 350°F. Bake for 45 minutes or until a toothpick inserted in the center of each loaf comes out clean. Cool on metal racks.

2 LOAVES

123

Herbed Focaccia

Focaccia used to be a rustic bread found all over Italy. Now it's a sophisticated bread found all over America.

> 1 packet active dry yeast (about 1 tablespoon)
> 1⅓ cups warm water
> 1 tablespoon extra virgin olive oil, plus more for oiling
> Salt
> 1¼ tablespoons minced fresh oregano
> 1¼ tablespoons minced fresh rosemary
> 1 tablespoon sun-dried tomatoes, packed in oil and drained
> 1½ cups whole wheat flour
> 1–1½ cups unbleached all-purpose flour

1. In a large bowl, dissolve the yeast in the water. Add the tablespoon of olive oil, salt to taste, 1 tablespoon of the oregano, 1 tablespoon of the rosemary, and the sun-dried tomatoes.
2. Stir in the whole wheat flour a half-cup at a time, beating until well blended. Stir in the all-purpose flour a half cup at a time until the mixture forms a ball.
3. Knead on a lightly floured surface for 10 minutes or until the dough is smooth and elastic. Form into a ball, place in an oiled bowl, and turn to cover the whole surface with oil.

4. Cover with a damp dish towel and let rise for 1–2 hours, or until it doubles in bulk. Punch down and knead a few times. Coat a 10-inch pie pan or 12-inch pizza pan with vegetable cooking spray and pat or roll the dough to fit the pan. Cover with a damp towel and let rise another 30 minutes.
5. Brush the dough with olive oil and scatter the remaining oregano and rosemary over the surface. In a preheated, 400°F oven, bake the focaccia for 25 minutes. Mist with water a few times during the first 15 minutes.
6. Cool on a rack. Serve warm or at room temperature.

1 LOAF

Grissini with Herbs

Bread sticks must be a first cousin to potato chips: It's hard to eat just one. These are crunchy through and through if you cook them 25 minutes, a bit softer at 20 minutes. Crispness also depends on how thinly they are rolled. The recipe makes four dozen, but they won't last long.

1 packet active dry yeast
    (about 1 tablespoon)
⅔ cup warm water
¼ cup extra virgin olive oil
1 teaspoon salt
1 tablespoon brown sugar

2¼ cups unbleached all-purpose flour
½ teaspoon white pepper
1 tablespoon minced fresh rosemary
1 tablespoon minced fresh sage
1 tablespoon minced fresh thyme
1 egg, beaten

1. In a large bowl, stir the yeast into the water and set aside for 4 minutes. Pour in the olive oil, salt, brown sugar, and 1 cup of the flour and beat about 100 strokes. The dough will be smooth but sticky.
2. Gradually add more flour until the dough is soft. If it is still wet, add more.
3. On a lightly floured surface, knead the dough until it is smooth and elastic. Place in the bowl, cover with plastic wrap, and put in a warm place to rise until it doubles in bulk (about 1½ hours).
4. Punch down the dough and split it in half. Shape each half like a little loaf, cut down the middle lengthwise with a sharp knife, and keep dividing the

pieces in half until you have 24. It doesn't matter whether they are all the same size or not. Repeat with the other loaf.

5. Mix the pepper with the herbs and spread the mixture on a piece of wax paper. Press the cut side of a dough stick into the herbs and then roll it out on a board with your fingers, spreading it into a pencil-sized shape. Place the "pencils" on a greased or nonstick cookie sheet about ½ inch apart, brush with the beaten egg, and cover with slightly oiled wax paper that does not actually touch the dough. Let rise a second time until they have nearly doubled in bulk (30 to 40 minutes).

6. Preheat the oven to 325°F, remove the paper, and bake until the sticks are golden brown.

7. Cool the bread sticks on a rack and store in an airtight container. They can be frozen.

4 DOZEN BREADSTICKS

Black Bread

The dark loaves found in Hungary, Ukraine, and Russia have a hearty, peasant quality. Here's one made darker with instant coffee and flavored with caraway seeds.

2 packets active dry yeast
     (about 2 tablespoons)
¼ cup warm water
¼ cup plus 1 tablespoon yellow
     cornmeal
¾ cup cold water
¾ cup boiling water
1 tablespoon salad oil, plus more
     for oiling

2 teaspoons salt
4 tablespoons molasses
1½ teaspoons caraway seeds
2 tablespoons plus 1 teaspoon
     instant coffee
1 cup wheat bran
2 cups rye flour
2 cups unbleached all-purpose flour

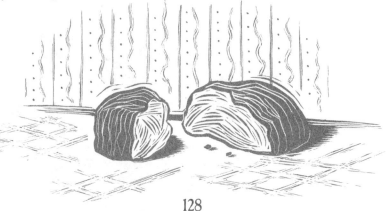

1. Dissolve the yeast in the warm water and set aside.
2. Add the cornmeal to the cold water and mix well. Pour the boiling water into a large bowl and add the cornmeal mixture, stirring until thick. Stir in the oil, salt, molasses, caraway seeds, and 2 tablespoons of the instant coffee.
3. Add the yeast mixture and blend in the wheat bran and flours, adding more water if needed. Stir. The dough should be fairly sticky.
4. Turn onto a lightly floured surface and knead, adding flour as necessary, until you have a firm, elastic dough. Place in an oiled bowl, turning it to grease the dough on all sides. Cover with a damp dish towel and let rise in a warm place until about double in bulk, about 1½ hours.
5. Punch down the dough, knead 2 or 3 minutes more on a lightly floured surface, and then divide in half. Shape the two halves into free-form ovals, cover with a damp dish towel, and let rise again until almost doubled in bulk, about 30 minutes.
6. Preheat the oven to 400°F. Mix the remaining teaspoon of instant coffee with hot water and brush the loaves. Place them on a greased baking sheet and bake for 40–45 minutes, or until the bread sounds hollow when tapped. Cool on a wire rack.

2 LOAVES

Cheese Dilly Bread

In word association, dill goes with pickles. But it has a wider world. For centuries in the Middle East, dill has been thought to have medicinal value. In cooking, it appears with potatoes, fish, and eggs and is one of the ingredients in curry powder. Here, it takes to bread.

3 cups unbleached all-purpose flour
1 cup whole wheat flour
1 tablespoon baking powder
1 teaspoon salt
2 tablespoons snipped fresh dill weed
½ teaspoon celery seeds
Freshly ground pepper
1½ cups shredded Monterey Jack cheese
1 small onion, finely chopped (⅓ cup)
1 egg
1¾ cups buttermilk

1. Preheat the oven to 375°F. Grease two 4 x 8-inch pans and set aside.
2. In a large bowl, combine the flours, baking powder, salt, dill, celery seeds, pepper to taste, cheese, and onion.

3. In another bowl, mix the egg and buttermilk and add to the dry ingredients, stirring just enough to combine.

4. Spoon the batter into the two pans and bake until a toothpick inserted in the center comes out clean (35 to 40 minutes). Cool in the pans for 10 minutes, then on a rack.

2 LOAVES

Potato Bread with Chives

Make mashed potatoes without the usual flavorings, and then make this bread — a solid loaf that toasts well and tastes good.

½ pound white potatoes (about 1 cup mashed)
1 cup potato water
2 packets active dry yeast (about 2 tablespoons)
2 tablespoons sugar
2 cups milk, warmed to the scalding point and cooled
3 tablespoons safflower or canola oil, plus more for oiling
3 teaspoons salt
8 cups unbleached all-purpose flour
2 tablespoons caraway seeds
3 tablespoons finely snipped fresh chives

1. Peel and boil the potatoes until tender. Drain, reserving a cup of the cooking water, and mash the potatoes. Set aside to cool.
2. Dissolve the yeast in the tepid potato water and let stand about 3 minutes. Add the mashed potatoes, sugar, milk, oil, salt, and 4 cups of the flour. Beat until smooth.
3. Add the caraway seeds and the rest of the flour, or as much as is needed to make a fairly stiff dough.
4. Sprinkle the chives over the dough. On a lightly floured surface, knead until it is smooth and elastic, at least 10 minutes. Place in an oiled bowl, turning to coat the dough on all sides, and let rise until doubled in bulk (about an hour).
5. Punch down the dough, knead a few times, and shape or braid into three loaves. Place in greased pans and let rise again until double in bulk.
6. Preheat the oven to 350°F. Bake for 40 minutes.

3 LOAVES

Chives have been a favorite herb in the Orient
for over 3,000 years.

Bread Bouquet Garni

Aromatic in the kitchen, tasty on the tongue, this bread contains a potpourri of herbs. If you happen to be missing one of them, substitute a favorite or double one of those listed. This is one for the bread machine and produces a large loaf.

¼ cup wheat bran
¼ cup rolled oats
2½ cups unbleached all-purpose bread flour
2 tablespoons powdered buttermilk
1 cup plus 2 tablespoons water
1 egg
2 tablespoons butter
½ teaspoon salt
½ teaspoon brown sugar
1 teaspoon minced fresh marjoram
1 teaspoon minced fresh thyme
1 teaspoon minced fresh rosemary
1 teaspoon minced fresh parsley
1 teaspoon freshly ground black pepper
Slightly less than 1 packet active dry yeast (2½ teaspoons)

1. Combine the wheat bran, rolled oats, bread flour, and buttermilk.
2. Place ingredients in your bread machine in the order prescribed by the instruction book.

1 LARGE LOAF

NOTE: *If you don't have a bread machine, you can certainly knead this combination of herbs into your favorite white or sourdough bread.*

Fruity Bread with Thyme

Lots of breads are called quick breads. This one is speed demon bread. It takes a half hour from start to finish because the cooking is done in the microwave.

2 cups sugar
1½ cups safflower or canola oil
3 eggs
1 teaspoon vanilla
2 cups fresh raspberries, mashed
1 tablespoon chopped fresh thyme
1 cup almonds, finely chopped
3 cups unbleached all-purpose flour
1 teaspoon salt
1 teaspoon baking soda
½ teaspoon nutmeg

1. Grease two 4 x 8-inch glass or microwave-safe loaf pans and set aside.
2. In a large mixing bowl, beat the sugar, oil, eggs, and vanilla.
3. Add the raspberries, thyme, and half the almonds.
4. Stir in the flour, salt, baking soda, and nutmeg. Divide the batter between the two pans. Sprinkle with the remainder of the chopped almonds.
5. Cover with wax paper and microwave one loaf at a time for 10 minutes at the half-power setting, then another 2 minutes at full power. When a toothpick inserted in the center comes out clean, the loaf is done.

2 LOAVES

Oats and Prunes Bread

Healthy is how this bread sounds. But it's good, too. Since it seems like a breakfast food, it's nice to know that it makes excellent toast.

2   cups pitted prunes, cut in thirds
½   cup orange juice
1   cup unbleached all-purpose flour
1   cup whole wheat flour
¾   cup rolled oats
¼   cup wheat bran
½   cup granulated sugar
¼   cup brown sugar
1   tablespoon baking powder
¼   teaspoon salt
½   teaspoon cinnamon
2   teaspoons minced fresh thyme
¾   cup buttermilk
2   eggs
¼   cup safflower or canola oil

1. Preheat the oven to 350°F. Combine the prunes with the orange juice and let soak while preparing the rest of the ingredients. Grease two 4 x 8-inch loaf pans and set aside.
2. In a large bowl, combine the flours, oats, wheat bran, sugars, baking powder, salt, cinnamon, and thyme.
3. In a second bowl, blend the buttermilk, eggs, and oil. Quickly stir the liquid mixture into the dry ingredients. Add the prunes and orange juice mixture and stir. Spoon the batter into the pans.
4. Bake for 40–45 minutes or until a toothpick inserted in the center comes out clean. Cool for 10 minutes in the pans, remove, and finish cooling on a rack.

2 LOAVES

Banana Lemon Balm Bread

When your child says "Are these rotten enough?" in the supermarket, you just hope the world knows you're getting ready to make banana bread. Of course, they're not actually rotten, but the bananas need to be painfully close to create a mellow banana bread.

1 ¾ cups unbleached all-purpose flour
¼ cup whole wheat flour
1 teaspoon baking soda
½ teaspoon salt
4 tablespoons butter, softened to room temperature
½ cup granulated sugar
½ cup light brown sugar
2 eggs, beaten
3 very ripe medium bananas
1 teaspoon minced fresh lemon balm
⅓ cup milk

1. Preheat the oven to 350°F. Butter a 4 x 8-inch loaf pan and line with wax paper.
2. Sift together the flours, baking soda, and salt.

3. In a large bowl, cream the butter and sugars together. Blend in the eggs, bananas, and lemon balm. Add half the flour mixture and half the milk, stirring. Add the rest of the milk and then the rest of the flour mixture, and blend well. Pour into the loaf pan.
4. Bake for an hour or until a toothpick inserted in the center comes out clean.

1 LOAF

Minted Apple Bread

Like most quick breads, this one freezes well. Applesauce gives it moisture, spearmint gives it tang.

2 cups unbleached all-purpose flour
¾ cup brown sugar
1 tablespoon baking powder
½ teaspoon baking soda
½ teaspoon salt
1 teaspoon cinnamon
2 tablespoons minced spearmint
1 egg
1 cup unsweetened applesauce
¼ cup safflower or canola oil

1. Preheat the oven to 350°F. Grease two 4 x 8-inch loaf pans and set aside.
2. In a large bowl, combine the flour, brown sugar, baking powder, baking soda, salt, and cinnamon.
3. In a small bowl, stir together the spearmint, egg, applesauce, and oil. Add to the dry ingredients. Stir until blended. Pour batter into loaf pans and bake for 45 minutes or until a toothpick inserted in the center comes out clean.

2 LOAVES

Spearmint, also known as "lamb mint," "pea mint,"
and "garden mint," is the mint most used
for culinary purposes.

Parsley Pine Nut Loaf

Pine nuts — *pignolia* in Italian — are sweet and crunchy. Added to this bread, along with fresh basil and parsley, they create a moist loaf that goes perfectly with a bowl of tomato soup.

3 cups unbleached all-purpose flour
1 medium white onion, minced
   (about ¾ cup)
2 tablespoons sugar
4 teaspoons baking powder
½ teaspoon baking soda
½ teaspoon salt
⅓ cup extra virgin olive oil

1 cup milk
2 eggs
1 tablespoon minced fresh basil
1 tablespoon minced fresh parsley
1 tablespoon grated Romano cheese
¾ cup peeled and grated zucchini
½ cup pine nuts, slightly chopped

1. Preheat the oven to 350°F. Grease two 4 x 8-inch loaf pans.
2. In a large bowl, combine the flour, onion, sugar, baking powder, baking soda, and salt. In another bowl, whisk the oil, milk, eggs, herbs, and cheese. Add the zucchini and pine nuts.
3. Stir the liquid mixture into the flour mixture, and then spoon the batter into the pans. Bake for 45 minutes or until a toothpick inserted in the center comes out clean. Cool for 10 minutes before removing from pans.

2 LOAVES

In the language of flowers, parsley stands for festivity, while basil represents good wishes.

Country Bread

Dried sage may have created a harsh memory, but fresh sage delights the palate.
Here it combines well with several kinds of flour for a peasant-style bread.

1 cup unbleached all-purpose flour
¼ cup whole wheat flour
½ cup cornmeal
2 tablespoons finely chopped fresh sage
2 teaspoons baking powder
½ teaspoon salt
  Freshly ground pepper
1 garlic clove, pressed
¼ cup olive oil
1 egg
½ cup buttermilk
¼ cup white wine

1. Preheat the oven to 350°F. Grease a shallow casserole or deep dish pie plate and set aside.
2. Combine the flours, cornmeal, sage, baking powder, salt, and pepper to taste.
3. Separately, whisk together the garlic, oil, egg, buttermilk, and wine. Fold the liquid mixture into the dry mixture and stir until combined.
4. Pour the batter into the casserole or pie plate and bake for 45 minutes or until a toothpick inserted in the center comes out clean. Cool for 10 minutes before removing from casserole.

1 LOAF

Sage was once believed to bestow immortality.

Pesto Roll

Basil came into its own when Americans began to substitute fresh green pesto sauce for the traditional red tomato sauce on their pasta. Now pesto goes into soups, onto pizza, or atop polenta. Here, it's rolled up inside a delicious eggy bread.

THE PESTO
½ cup olive oil
¼ cup grated Romano and Parmesan cheese
2 tablespoons pine nuts
1 cup basil leaves
1 cup parsley, stems removed
Juice of 1 lemon

FOR THE ROLL
4 tablespoons butter
½ cup unbleached all-purpose flour
2 cups milk
Salt and freshly ground pepper
5 eggs, separated

FOR THE FILLING
Pesto
2 cups ricotta cheese
2 tablespoons shredded
   mozzarella cheese

1. Combine all the pesto ingredients in a blender or food processor.
2. Preheat the oven to 400°F. Grease an 11 x 16-inch jelly roll pan, line with parchment paper, oil the paper, and sprinkle with flour.

3. Melt the butter in a saucepan, remove from the stove, and stir in the flour. Add the milk and cook until boiling, stirring constantly. Simmer for 2 minutes, then add salt and pepper to taste.
4. Beat in the egg yolks one at a time. Beat the egg whites until they stand in soft peaks; fold into the white sauce. Spread the mixture in the jelly roll pan. Bake for 30 minutes.
5. When the roll is done, turn it out on a clean dish towel on a flat surface. To add the filling, spread the roll with a layer of pesto followed by an extra layer of ricotta. Starting on the long side, roll the whole thing up. Sprinkle with shredded mozzarella and return to the oven to keep warm and to melt the cheese. Cut into thick slices.

6 SERVINGS

Delicious Dumplings

Called *gnocchi* in Italy and *spaetzle* in Germany, European dumplings come in a variety of shapes and sizes. These are Eastern European and are perfect in chicken soup or with a cream gravy.

6 shallots, minced (3 tablespoons)
3 tablespoons butter
3½ cups cubed white bread, crusts removed
2 eggs
¾ cup milk
2 tablespoons finely chopped parsley
½ teaspoon salt
2 cups unbleached all-purpose flour

1. Cook the shallots in the butter until golden and soft. Add the bread cubes and cook until they start to brown. Cool.
2. In a large bowl, combine the eggs, milk, parsley, and salt. Stir in the bread and shallots mixture and let stand for 5 minutes.
3. Stir in enough of the flour to make a soft, slightly sticky dough. In a soup pot, heat about 2 quarts of water to a boil. With flour-covered fingers, shape the dough into 1-inch balls and drop, one at a time, into the boiling water.

4. Simmer uncovered until the dumplings rise to the surface, stirring occasionally to make sure none are stuck to the pot. Simmer another 6 minutes. Remove the dumplings with a slotted spoon or Chinese strainer.

25–30 ONE-INCH DUMPLINGS

Cranberry Fritters

Like French cheeses, fritters seem to stake out regional territories. Some places you find them with clams, other places with corn. Here the deep-fried delectables come with cranberries for tartness and rosemary for fragrance.

2   cups raw cranberries
2   eggs
6   tablespoons honey
2   tablespoons melted unsalted butter
2   teaspoons orange zest
2   teaspoons minced fresh rosemary leaves
1 ¼   cups unbleached all-purpose flour
¼   teaspoon salt
2   teaspoons baking powder
Powdered sugar for topping

1. Wash, sort, and coarsely chop the cranberries. Cook in enough water to cover them until just soft — they'll start to pop at that point. Drain well and spread out on paper towels.
2. In a large bowl, beat the eggs, add the honey, and continue beating. Beat in the butter, orange zest, and rosemary. Stir in the cranberries.

3. Sift the flour, salt, and baking powder together. Add to the cranberry mixture and blend gently.
4. Drop the batter from a teaspoon into deep fat that has been preheated to between 350°F and 365°F. Use a candy thermometer to maintain the right temperature.
5. Fry a few fritters at a time until they are golden brown, about 3–4 minutes. Remove with a slotted spoon and drain on paper towels.
6. Test the first few fritters to make sure they are moist but not runny. Sift powdered sugar over them and serve warm. They will keep in a low oven for a while, if necessary.

ABOUT 18 FRITTERS

153

Apple Sage Stuffing

The aroma of Thanksgiving, hours before dinner is served, holds people hostage, not only on the holiday itself but in memory as well. Early in the morning, the stuffing gets the holiday started, sending a smell of butter, garlic, and onions through the house. Here's one way to fill up the turkey cavity and wake the hungry.

6 tablespoons butter
1 stalk celery with leaves, chopped (about ½ cup)
2 garlic cloves, mashed
2 medium onions, chopped (about 1 cup)
1 large apple, peeled and chopped (about 1 cup)
4 cups bread cubes
1 cup hot water
2 eggs, beaten
1 tablespoon minced fresh sage
1 tablespoon minced fresh thyme
1 teaspoon salt
Freshly ground pepper

1. In a deep skillet, melt the butter and sauté the celery, garlic, and onions until soft but not browned. Add the apple and stir for about 2 minutes.
2. Remove from heat. In a large bowl, combine the apple mixture with the bread cubes, hot water, eggs, sage, and thyme.
3. Stir until well blended, adding more hot water if needed. The stuffing should be moist but not wet. Add the salt and the pepper to taste.

ENOUGH STUFFING FOR A 14-POUND TURKEY

Zucchini Cornbread

When you are overwhelmed with zucchini and underwhelmed with ideas, this recipe will help use up quite a few of the infamous green summer squash. If they've hidden under the vines and gotten big enough to make a dugout canoe, don't despair — peel off the tough skin and grate the rest.

3 or 4 *zucchinis, grated (about 6 cups)*
2 *teaspoons salt*
2 *cups cornmeal*
1 *cup unbleached all-purpose flour*
1 *tablespoon baking powder*
3 *eggs, beaten*
2 *tablespoons honey*
1½ *cups buttermilk*
2 *tablespoons minced fresh oregano*

1. Preheat the oven to 350°F. Place the zucchini in a colander and toss with 1 teaspoon of the salt to draw out some of the liquid. Let drain about 30 minutes.
2. Sift together the cornmeal, flour, baking powder, and the rest of the salt.
3. Mix the eggs, honey, buttermilk, and oregano. Combine with the dry ingredients.

4. Rinse the salt from the zucchini and squeeze out the water. You will have about 3 cups of pulp. Stir into the batter.
5. Pour the batter into a 9-inch springform pan or two small loaf pans and bake for 40 minutes. Cool for about 10 minutes before removing from pans.

8–10 SERVINGS

Quesadillas with Tortillas de Harina

Quesadillas can be lunch or surprising hors d'oeuvres. Tortillas can be purchased in most groceries, but they can also be made at home. These are the flour tortillas of Mexico — soft and nearly white. Many Mexican women still pat them into rounds with their hands, but they can also be made with a tortilla press — or just rolled with a rolling pin.

TORTILLA INGREDIENTS
- 4 cups unbleached all-purpose flour
- 2 teaspoons salt
- ⅓ cup shortening
- 1 cup warm water

1. Sift the flour and salt together and work the shortening in with the fingertips or blend it quickly in a food processor, being careful not to overblend. Stir in enough water to form a firm ball, adding extra if needed. Knead well.
2. Form balls about the size of an egg, and roll between well-oiled sheets of wax paper into 8-inch circles. The tortillas should be fairly thin. Cook on a medium-hot griddle, 2 minutes on the first side and only a minute on the second.

Quesadilla Filling

- 1 cup shredded Monterey Jack cheese
- 1 cup shredded sharp cheddar cheese
- 2 tomatoes, seeded, drained, and diced
- 2 tablespoons chopped fresh oregano
- 4 tablespoons chopped fresh parsley
- 1 teaspoon cumin

1. Place a flour tortilla on a cookie sheet. Scatter some cheese, tomatoes, oregano, parsley, and cumin on it, staying a quarter inch away from the edge. Put another tortilla on top and repeat the layer of cheese, tomatoes, and herbs. Top with a third tortilla.

2. Repeat the process with three more tortillas until all the ingredients have been used. Bake in a 400°F oven for 6–8 minutes. Cut into wedges and serve hot.

AT LEAST 3 STACKS, 6–8 PIECES EACH

Bruschetta

When you soak your fresh Italian bread in olive oil laced with garlic, you're partaking not only of a tempting appetizer but of a centuries-old practice. In ancient Rome, the first taste of freshly pressed, green olive oil was from an oil-soaked piece of bread. In recent years, bruschetta has become fashionable in better Italian restaurants. Here's a version you can try for yourself.

8 slices of Italian bread
4 large garlic cloves, peeled and sliced in half
½ cup olive oil, as green as possible
1 teaspoon freshly ground pepper

1. Toast the bread.
2. While it is hot, rub one side with garlic.
3. Serve the toast garlic side up, with olive oil on the side. Guests can spoon olive oil over their toast slices, add a couple of twists of the pepper grinder, and enjoy being with-it — and with the centuries.

4 SERVINGS

Catalan Classic

Thousands of Americans had their first taste of tomato bread at the 1992 Olympic Games in Barcelona, center of Spain's Catalan culture. It is simple but seductive.

　　　1　*loaf crusty bread, cut in half lengthwise*
　3–4　*garlic cloves, sliced in half*
　　　4　*ripe tomatoes*
　　　　Spanish olive oil
　　　　Salt
　　　　Sweet white onion for garnish (optional)
　　　　Pitted black olives for garnish (optional)

1.　Rub the cut side of the bread with the garlic cloves, then cut each half crosswise into inch-thick pieces. Brown the bread under the broiler, being careful not to burn it.
2.　Cut the tomatoes in half and rub the toasted bread with the tomato, letting the pulp sink in. Discard the skin. Dribble olive oil over the tomato bread and sprinkle lightly with salt to taste.
3.　Serve immediately as is, or garnish with a slice of onion and an olive.

4–6 SERVINGS

Sesame Rounds

It may seem absurd — given all the variety available at the supermarket — to make crackers, but it's not. Try these and see.

> 1 cup sesame seeds
> 2 cups unbleached all-purpose flour
> 1 teaspoon salt
> Dash cayenne
> 12 tablespoons butter
> ¼ cup ice water
> 1 tablespoon minced fresh parsley, washed and dried

1. Preheat the oven to 300°F. In a dry skillet, brown the sesame seeds, stirring so they don't burn.
2. In a bowl, combine the flour, salt, and cayenne. Cut in the butter. Add the ice water a tablespoon at a time. Add the sesame seeds.
3. Roll the dough to ¼-inch thickness. Sprinkle evenly with the parsley and give it another quick roll. Cut into small rounds, 1½ inches across. Bake 30 minutes or until lightly brown.
4. Cool on a rack and store in a tightly closed container.

24 CRACKERS

Provence Spread

Top quality olive oil is the ticket here. Don't look at the unit price; just keep tasting until you find a fine olive oil that you like. Some chefs swear by Spanish olive oil, while others use only Italian. Saying they are all alike is like saying all potatoes are the same.

> ½ cup pitted black olives
> ½ cup pitted green olives
> ¾ cup extra virgin olive oil
> 6 garlic cloves
> 2 tablespoons capers
> *Juice of ½ small lemon (2 teaspoons)*
> *Salt and freshly ground pepper*
> *Crusty Italian or French bread*

1. Finely chop enough black olives to make 1 tablespoon. Do the same with the green, mix the two, and set aside.
2. Pour the oil into a blender and add the garlic, capers, and lemon juice. Blend until almost smooth.
3. Put the oil mixture into a small bowl and stir in the chopped olives. Add salt and pepper to taste.
4. Spread on thin slices of toast made with crusty bread.

1 CUP

Herb Cheese Spread

Cooks usually want their families to wait until fresh loaves of bread cool before they are cut. But everyone knows a warm loaf melts the butter — or this cheesy mix. Try it on a crusty heel of whole wheat or oatmeal, five minutes out of the oven.

8 tablespoons butter, softened
3 cups grated cheddar cheese
2 tablespoons finely snipped fresh chives
1 tablespoon caraway seeds
2 tablespoons cognac

1. Beat the butter and cheese together.
2. Blend in the chives, caraway seeds, and cognac.

ABOUT 2 CUPS

164

Mustard Spread

Add a little spice to bread or crackers with this smooth, herbed spread.

> 8 *tablespoons butter, softened*
> 1 *tablespoon finely chopped fresh parsley*
> 1 *tablespoon finely chopped fresh basil*
> 1 *tablespoon spicy mustard*
> *Bread or crackers*

1. Using an electric mixer or a food processor, cream the ingredients together.
2. Spread on bread or crackers. It will keep in the refrigerator for several weeks.

ABOUT ½ CUP

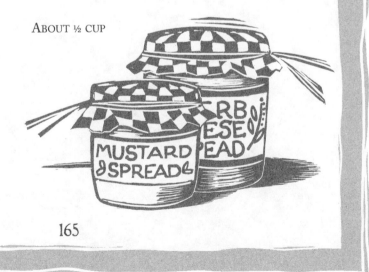

HERBAL SWEETS

Sweet Lemon Bars

Sweet lemon may be an oxymoron, but it works. These sugary confections, flavored with lemon juice and lemon thyme, tempt the palate with their sweet-tart taste.

½ cup butter
¼ cup confectioners' sugar
1 cup unbleached flour, sifted
2 eggs
1 cup granulated sugar
½ teaspoon baking powder
¼ teaspoon salt
Juice of 1 large lemon
1 teaspoon fresh minced lemon thyme or ½ teaspoon dried

1. Preheat the oven to 350°F. Cream the butter and sugar. Add the sifted flour, blending smoothly. Using your fingers, press the mixture into an 8 x 8-inch pan. Bake 20 minutes.
2. Beat together the eggs, sugar, baking powder, salt, lemon juice, and lemon thyme. Pour over the crust and bake another 20 minutes.
3. Cool, then cut into squares.

16 BARS

Lemon Thyme Cookies

When time is a problem, cookies that can be made over two days may help with the daily race against the clock. These have the fragrance of thyme as well — in this case lemon thyme, just one of some 350 species of this perennial, which often works nicely as a decorative plant in a rock or container garden. If lemon thyme is hard to come by, substitute another kind.

> 1 cup butter or margarine, softened
> 1½ cups granulated sugar
> 2 eggs
> 2½ cups unbleached flour
> 1 teaspoon cream of tartar
> ½ teaspoon salt
> 5 tablespoons finely chopped fresh lemon thyme or
>   3 tablespoons dried

1. Cream the butter with the sugar, add the eggs, and mix well.
2. Sift together the flour, cream of tartar, and salt. Stir the flour mixture into the butter, sugar, and eggs until well blended, then add the lemon thyme.
3. Chill overnight or until firm enough to roll.
4. Preheat the oven to 350°F. Roll the chilled dough into 1-inch balls and bake on a greased cookie sheet for 10 minutes.

4 DOZEN COOKIES

Thyme was once thought to relieve
epilepsy and melancholy.

Crisp Caraway Cookies

Caraway seeds bring a distinctive taste to many breads, cakes, and cookies, especially in the cuisine of northern and eastern Europe. The mild-tasting leaves of the plant, usually used in soups, are less common than the crunchy seeds. For a different taste, substitute poppy seeds here.

1⅔ cups unbleached flour
1 teaspoon baking powder
¼ teaspoon baking soda
¼ teaspoon salt
2 teaspoons caraway seeds
½ cup butter or margarine, softened
⅔ cup granulated sugar
2 eggs
½ teaspoon vanilla extract

1. Preheat the oven to 375°F.
2. Mix together flour, baking powder, baking soda, salt, and caraway seeds. Set aside.
3. Cream the butter and sugar until fluffy. Add the eggs and vanilla and beat well.

4. Stir in the flour mixture. Wrap the dough in plastic wrap and chill several hours, overnight, or until firm enough to roll (the dough will still be rather soft).
5. Cut the dough into quarters. Work with one quarter at a time, keeping the rest in the refrigerator. Roll the dough very thin on a floured surface. (Use a pastry cloth and covered rolling pin to prevent the dough from sticking.) Cut with a floured 3-inch round cutter. Put on ungreased cookie sheets.
6. Bake on the top rack of oven 8 to 10 minutes, watching closely. Remove to a wire rack to cool. Repeat until the dough is gone. Store in an airtight container or freezer.

4 DOZEN COOKIES

According to folklore, caraway has the power to cure hysterics and to keep lovers true.

Anise Bars

A licorice-like flavor emanates from anise, which is actually a member of the parsley family. From its small yellowish white flowers come anise seeds and oil. (If you can't find anise oil, you can make your own by combining a tablespoon of anise seeds with a half cup of salad oil in a sterilized bottle and letting the mixture stand in the refrigerator for a week before using. For a stronger flavor, just increase the proportion of anise seeds.)

  2 cups unbleached flour
  1 teaspoon baking powder
  ¾ cup granulated sugar
  ¼ cup butter
  2 eggs, beaten
1½ drops anise oil
  1 teaspoon anise seeds
  ¼ cup butter or margarine, melted

1. Preheat the oven to 375°F.
2. In a food processor, blend flour, baking powder, and sugar. Cut butter into half-inch chunks and add to the flour mixture. Blend briefly. The mixture will not be smooth. Add the eggs and anise oil, and blend for two seconds or until smooth.

3. Cut the dough in half. Roll out one piece to ¼-inch thick and then cut into sticks about 3½ inches long and ½ inch wide. If you use a zigzag cutter, you'll get a pretty, crimped edge. Place the bars on ungreased baking sheets.
4. Add the anise seeds to the melted butter or margarine, and brush on lightly with a pastry brush. Bake 10 minutes and cool on a rack.

2 DOZEN BARS

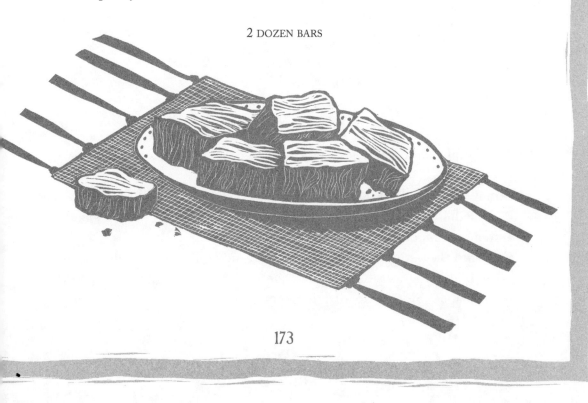

Old-Fashioned Herbed Candies

Penny candies in the old-fashioned general store were often made with combinations of herbs, and some tasted more hot than sweet, more bitter than refreshing. Here's a recipe that can be adapted to fit everyone's taste.

Herbs to try include peppermint, horehound, spearmint, orangemint, applemint, wintergreen, lemon verbena, and lemon catnip. For variation, add 1 tablespoon mint leaves or 1 teaspoon crushed anise seeds to horehound for a horehound candy.

4 cups boiling water
2 cups herb leaves with stems and blossoms
3 cups granulated sugar
3 cups brown sugar
½ tablespoon butter

1. Pour boiling water over the leaves and steep for 10 minutes, longer for stronger tea. Meanwhile, butter a shallow pan.
2. Strain the leaves, add the sugars and butter to the tea, and bring it to a boil over medium heat. Continue boiling until syrup hardens when a small amount is dropped into cold water.
3. Pour into the buttered pan and score the candy into squares before it sets, or break it up into pieces as soon as it hardens. Wrap each hardened piece in waxed paper. Store in an airtight container.

175

Frosted Lavender Sticks

The somewhat floppy, gray-green lavender leaves and purple flowers create a soft corner in the herb garden. Sugared, the flowers are a crisply pretty nibble. You should be sure the plants have not been sprayed with herbicides or pesticides. For variety, substitute violets or rose petals for the lavender.

12 *stalks fresh lavender flowers*
1 *egg white, beaten until frothy*
½ *cup granulated sugar*

1. Dip the flowers of the lavender stalks in egg white, then roll in or dust with sugar. If you are worried about eating uncooked egg whites, substitute the proper amount of pasteurized, dried egg whites, which are available in most supermarkets.
2. Air dry on waxed paper.

1 DOZEN STICKS

Rose Geranium Syrup

Another interesting sauce for ice cream — or a marinade for fruits — is this flowery syrup, which can be made ahead of time and stored in sterilized jars.

> 2½ *cups water*
> 2 *cups sugar*
> 1 *handful rose geranium leaves*

1. Place the water and sugar in a deep saucepan, and stir until dissolved.
2. Heat to a boil and let boil for 5 minutes without stirring. Remove from heat, add the rose geranium leaves, cover, and steep for 10 minutes.
3. Strain the syrup into a clean pan and boil for 30 seconds. Remove from heat. Pour into jars that have been sterilized. The syrup keeps 6 to 9 months in the refrigerator.

4–5 HALF-PINT JARS

In the language of flowers,
rose geranium represents "preference."

Shortbread Cookies with Thyme

"Parsley, sage, rosemary and thyme," sang Simon and Garfunkel, flavoring the music of a generation. Just two of their four herbs create rich harmony here. If you use dried herbs, use half as much.

½   *cup plus 1 tablespoon butter*
¼   *cup confectioners' sugar*
1½ *cups flour*
1   *teaspoon lemon zest*
2   *teaspoons minced fresh rosemary*
2   *teaspoons minced fresh thyme*
Extra confectioners' sugar

1. Cream the butter and sugar together by hand or in a food processor. Add the flour, lemon zest, rosemary, and thyme. Knead gently to make a soft dough and chill for an hour.
2. Preheat the oven to 350°F. Roll the dough on a pastry cloth or lightly floured surface about ⅜ inch thick and cut into diamonds, circles, or free forms. Pinching the edges, pie fashion, will create an attractive crinkle.

3. Place the cookies on a greased cookie sheet. Bake for 15 to 20 minutes or until the cookies are lightly golden. It is important not to overbake.
4. Sprinkle lightly with the extra confectioners' sugar while the cookies are hot. Cool on a rack.

2–3 DOZEN COOKIES, DEPENDING ON THE CUTS

Pungent Minty Tea

This tea, an old-fashioned recipe, lets the mint bite. Delicious served hot, it also makes a wonderfully refreshing iced tea.

4 cups boiling water
3 tablespoons tea leaves
½ cup freshly chopped mint leaves

1. Pour the boiling water over the tea leaves and steep until it reaches desired strength. Strain.
2. Pour the hot tea over the mint leaves and steep 1 minute. Strain and serve. For iced tea, let cool and pour over ice cubes.

2 SERVINGS

180

Grandma's Iced Tea

When the scent of fresh-mown hay comes from the fields, and July days are hot and humid, a tall glass of this tea, served with lunch or in the shade of an old tree by the pond, cools the palate. It's also good while you're relaxing in a wicker loveseat on the porch.

> 5 *teaspoons orange pekoe tea*
> 10 *heaping tablespoons granulated sugar*
> 2 *tablespoons chopped fresh spearmint*
> *Juice and rind of one orange*
> *Juice and rind of one lemon*
> 4 *cups boiling water*
> *Cold water*

1. Put the tea in a strainer and pour boiling water over it into the sugar, spearmint, and fruit juice and rinds. Keep dipping the strainer into the liquid until it is a medium brown color.
2. Add enough cold water to make 2 quarts. Remove the fruit rinds before serving.

2 QUARTS

Peppermint Angel Food Cake

Angel food cake is an American favorite. This one has a peppermint twist. For a special occasion, serve with peppermint stick ice cream and a spot of chocolate sauce. Or serve it plain, garnished with a sprig of fresh mint.

1 cup cake flour
2 tablespoons cornstarch
¾ cup granulated sugar
5 large egg whites
½ teaspoon vanilla extract
1 tablespoon finely chopped fresh peppermint

1. Preheat the oven to 350°F. Use nonstick baking paper to line the base of an ungreased angel food cake pan.
2. Sift together the flour, the cornstarch, and 1 tablespoon of the sugar.
3. Beat the egg whites until stiff. Use a whisk to gradually add the rest of the sugar, continuing to whisk the mixture until very thick.
4. Fold in the flour mixture, vanilla, and mint. Turn into the pan and bake 35 to 40 minutes.
5. Invert the cake, still in the pan, over a tray of ice cubes to cool. Do not unmold until cold. Serve drizzled with Minted Chocolate Sauce, if desired (page 184).

6 SERVINGS

Black-stemmed peppermint has the strongest flavor.

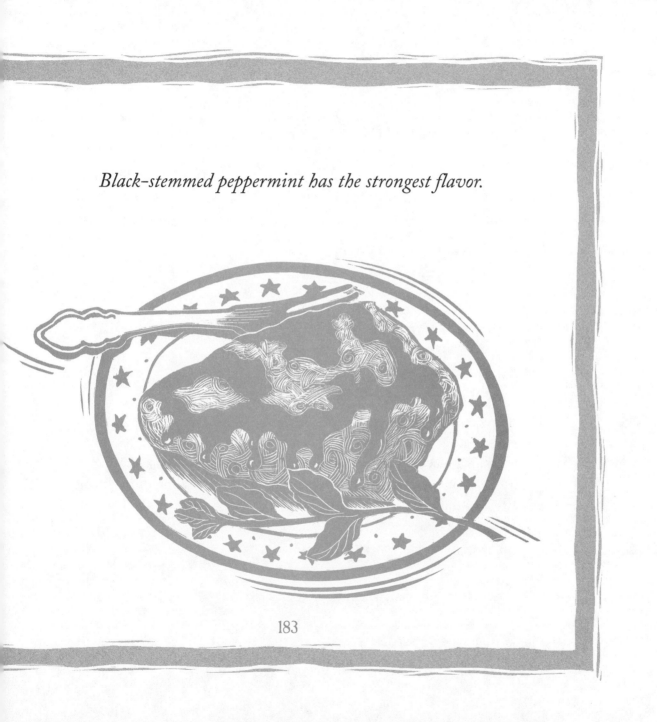

Minted Chocolate Sauce

To put a little zip into traditional chocolate sauce, add a little mint. The quick way is to add a few drops of peppermint extract to the chocolate sauce. Only slightly longer to prepare is the following sauce made with fresh mint.

½ cup water
½ cup coarsely chopped fresh mint leaves, crushed
3 squares unsweetened chocolate
¾ cup sugar
¼ teaspoon salt
4½ tablespoons butter or margarine
½ teaspoon vanilla extract
½ cup water

1. Boil ¼ cup of the water and pour over the mint leaves in a small bowl. Let stand for 10 minutes.
2. In a small saucepan, melt the chocolate in the other ¼ cup of water. (Or combine and heat in the microwave oven about 2 minutes, stirring after 1 minute.)

3. Strain the mint-flavored water into a small saucepan with the melted chocolate, sugar, and salt. Cook, stirring, about 5 minutes or until the sugar melts and the mixture thickens.
4. Stir in the butter and vanilla and continue heating until the butter melts. Serve hot or cold.

1¼ CUPS

Mints have been used medicinally
for more than 5,000 years.

Lemon Cheesecake

Calendulas are an intrepid summer annual, brightly coloring the garden through rain, drought, heat, and even the coolness of fall. Sometimes called pot marigold, calendula is often used as a way to add color to cheese or cakes — even to fabric. Finely ground calendula petals can be added to this cheesecake for color and a few petals or blossoms used as a garnish on each serving.

   6 *eggs, separated*
   ½ *cup plus 2 tablespoons butter*
   ½ *cup plus 2 tablespoons sugar*
  12 *ounces softened cream cheese*
   4 *teaspoons chopped fresh lemon balm or 2 teaspoons dried*
   4 *teaspoons lemon zest*
   2 *teaspoons finely ground calendula petals (optional)*

*In the language of flowers,
lemon balm stands for sympathy.*

1. Preheat the oven to 325°F.
2. In a small mixer bowl, beat the egg whites until they stand in soft peaks.
3. In another bowl, cream the butter, sugar, egg yolks, and cream cheese. Add the lemon balm, lemon zest, and petals to the butter mixture. Fold in the beaten egg whites.
4. Place in a greased angel food tube pan and bake 55 minutes. Cool 10 minutes before inverting on plate.

10 SERVINGS

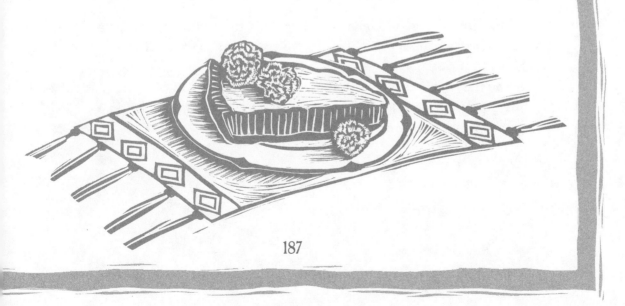

Maple Sage Apple Cake

Usually you put maple syrup on your pancakes and sage in the Thanksgiving turkey stuffing. This time they are teamed up in a beautiful, dark cake made in a shaped pan lined with apple slices and flavored with applesauce. For the full taste, use real maple syrup — blends don't have the same effect.

MAPLE SAGE APPLESAUCE

3 or 4 tart, crisp apples
2 tablespoons maple syrup
2 sage leaves
1 tablespoon water
Juice of half a lemon

1. Peel, core, and cut-up the apples. Combine them with the syrup and sage leaves in a small saucepan. Add a tablespoon or so of water to prevent sticking.
2. Keep the heat low and cook until the apples are soft. Remove the sage, add the lemon juice, and whip with a wire whisk until smooth.

MAPLE SAGE APPLE CAKE

⅞ cup butter
2 cups unbleached flour
1 teaspoon baking soda
1 teaspoon baking powder
½ teaspoon salt
1 teaspoon cinnamon
1 cup plus 4 tablespoons packed
   dark brown sugar

2 eggs
1 tablespoon minced fresh sage
1 cup Maple Sage Applesauce
2 large apples (Cortland, Mutsu, or
   Spy), peeled, quartered, and cored
Juice of half a lemon

1. Preheat the oven to 350°F. Use 2 tablespoons of the butter to generously grease the bottom and sides of a 9½-inch bundt pan.
2. Sift the flour with the baking soda, baking powder, salt, and cinnamon.
3. Cream 1 cup of the brown sugar and the remainder of the butter, or combine quickly in a food processor. Blend in the eggs. Add the minced sage and the Maple Sage Applesauce to the sugar mixture and process or beat well.
4. Gradually add the flour mixture to the applesauce mixture, blending well.
5. Slice the apples thinly and toss with the lemon juice. Sprinkle the extra 4 tablespoons of brown sugar over the buttered surfaces of the bundt pan and arrange the apple slices around the bottom and sides of the pan.
6. Pour the batter into the pan, taking care not to disturb the apple slices. Bake 50 to 60 minutes, until the top is golden brown and a cake tester or toothpick comes out clean. Cool to room temperature on a rack before taking the cake out of the pan. Loosen, then invert the glossy cake on a plate.

8–10 SERVINGS

Lemon Sponge with Rosemary

This classy dessert combines the sharpness of lemon with rosemary, the herb that makes noses wiggle in the kitchen and insists on being noticed in any dish. Be sure to remove all the stems and to mince the rosemary as finely as possible. It's a tough-leaved herb, and while it's traditionally associated with remembrance, it ought to be as subtle as possible here.

> 1 cup sugar
> 3 tablespoons flour
> 2 eggs, separated
> Juice and zest of a large lemon
> 1 tablespoon melted butter or margarine
> ⅛ teaspoon salt
> 1 teaspoon finely chopped fresh rosemary
> 1 cup milk
> Rosemary sprigs for garnish

1. Heat the oven to 350°F.
2. Mix the sugar and flour. Beat the egg yolks and add them, along with the lemon juice and zest, butter, salt, and rosemary, to the sugar and flour.
3. Stir in the milk. Beat the egg whites until they stand in soft peaks, and add to the mixture.

4. Pour into a casserole dish or into individual custard cups. Set in a large pan containing an inch of hot water and bake for 30 to 40 minutes. The top should be slightly browned. Additional rosemary sprigs may be used for garnish.

6 SERVINGS

Raspberry Peach Tart

Ever since someone invented Peach Melba, the world has known that raspberries and peaches are a fit. In this case, they are equal partners, housed in a crunchy graham cracker crust.

3 *medium fresh peaches*
¼ *teaspoon lemon juice*
1 *cup fresh raspberries*
2 *cups plain yogurt*
4 *tablespoons confectioners' sugar*
2 *teaspoons chopped fresh mint*
9-inch graham cracker crust
2 *teaspoons granulated sugar*

1. Coarsely chop 2 peaches and sprinkle with lemon juice to keep them from turning brown. Gently wash the raspberries and combine with the peaches.
2. Stir half the yogurt, sugar, and mint together and spread in the 9-inch graham cracker crust. Arrange the fruit over the yogurt mixture, cover with plastic wrap, and refrigerate for an hour.

3. Just before serving, stir the 2 teaspoons of sugar into the rest of the yogurt and put a dollop on each section of the tart. Slice the remaining peach and arrange on top to garnish.

6 SERVINGS

Tangerine Cooler

Sweet tangerines, lime-green kiwis with their distinctive black seeds, bananas, and orange juice blend in a fruit drink that will cut the thirst created by a summer day.

2 tangerines, peeled, sectioned, and trimmed
2 ripe kiwifruit, peeled and sliced
2 bananas, peeled and sliced
1 cup orange juice
2 tablespoons chopped fresh mint, plus four sprigs
   for garnish
Crushed ice

1. Chill four tall glasses in the freezer.
2. In a blender, combine the tangerines, kiwifruit, bananas, orange juice, and chopped mint. Purée.
3. Fill the chilled glasses with crushed ice and add the fruit mixture. Garnish each drink with a mint sprig and serve.

4 SERVINGS

194

Rosemary Fruit Punch

Herbs put both fragrance and punch into the punch. For a delicious golden brew, try this — either well-chilled for summer or hot for a fireside party in the winter.

> 1 can pineapple juice (46 ounces)
> 5 sprigs fresh rosemary or 1 tablespoon dried
> ½ cup sugar
> Juice of 8 lemons (about 1½ cups)
> 1½ cups cranberry juice
> 2 cups water
> 1 quart ginger ale
> Paper-thin lemon slices for garnish

1. In a small saucepan, heat 1 cup of pineapple juice until it boils. Remove from heat, add the rosemary, and steep 8 to 10 minutes.
2. Dissolve the sugar in the hot juice and then strain into a pitcher containing the remaining pineapple juice, lemon juice, cranberry juice, and water. Chill, if serving cold.
3. Just before serving, add the ginger ale and garnish with the lemon slices.

3¾ QUARTS

Lavender Ice Cream

In fiction, lavender goes with old lace, and in ice cream, it exudes elegance as well. This ice cream, from Jane Newdick's *At Home with Herbs,* is easy to make and should be served with miniature macaroons or vanilla wafers. Flower heads, of course, must be unsprayed.

> 4 egg yolks
> ¾ cup sugar
> ⅔ cup half-and-half
> 6 fresh lavender flower heads
> ⅔ cup whipping or heavy cream

1. Whisk the egg yolks and sugar together until light and foamy. In a saucepan, gently heat the half-and-half with the lavender flowers. Bring to a boil, then strain into the egg yolk mixture.
2. Return the mixture to the stove and cook over very low heat, stirring constantly until it is slightly thickened and coats the back of a spoon. Do not let it boil. Pour the custard into a bowl, and refrigerate until it is really cold.

3. Whip the cream until it forms peaks. Fold into the cold custard.
   Process in an ice-cream maker or freeze in a container.

4 SERVINGS

Lemon Thyme Sorbet

Thyme, examined closely, has the tiniest of leaves and shrubby little stems. In fact, it's sometimes called a shrublet. So make sure it's just the leaves you're chopping, not the stalks, when you're adding this lemony herb to what could be a perfect entremets — this palate-clearing sorbet.

½ cup sugar
1½ cups water
　 Juice and thinly pared rinds of two lemons
4 tablespoons fresh lemon thyme leaves
1 egg white or an equal amount of pasteurized, dried egg whites

1. Heat the sugar, water, and lemon rinds in a heavy-bottomed saucepan, allowing the sugar to dissolve without stirring. If crystals start to form on the sides of the pan, brush them down into the liquid with a wet pastry brush.
2. Bring to a boil and boil briskly for 5 minutes. Remove the pan from the heat, and dip the base briefly in cold water to stop the cooking process. Add the thyme leaves to the syrup and let cool completely.
3. When cooled, strain off the leaves and rinds and add the lemon juice. Process in an ice-cream freezer. When the mixture is nearly frozen, beat the egg white until it stands in soft peaks and add to the mixture for a sorbet with a smooth texture.

4 SERVINGS

Rose Petal Ice Cream

For delicacy, the shell-pink color of this ice cream and its faint scent of roses are an unbeatable combination. Serve in a tall sherbet glass or fluted pastry shell. Use highly scented red rose petals from a plant that has not been sprayed with pesticides or herbicides.

> 1 cup whipping cream
> 1 cup half-and-half
> Petals of 4 scented roses
> 2 egg yolks
> ¾ cup sugar
> ¼ teaspoon vanilla extract
> 2 teaspoons honey

1. In a saucepan, heat the cream, half-and-half, and rose petals almost to the boiling point, removing from the heat just before the mixture boils. Cover and let sit until cool.
2. In a large mixing bowl, whisk together egg yolks, sugar, vanilla, and honey until creamy. Strain the rose-flavored cream mixture into the egg mixture and stir. Pour into a double boiler and cook until slightly thickened, but do not let it boil.

3. Chill the custard mixture, then freeze it or process it in an ice-cream maker. Store in the freezer. Let it soften about 20 minutes before serving.

4–6 SERVINGS

Lime-Mint Sherbet

For a refreshing dessert, topped perhaps with a bit of Minted Chocolate Sauce (page 184), try this sherbet. Hint: The rinds of lemons and limes can be harvested easily for zest if you get a small tool called a lemon zester from your kitchenware shop.

> 12 *sprigs fresh mint*
> 2 *cups water*
> ¾ *cup granulated sugar*
> ½ *cup light corn syrup*
> 2 *teaspoons lime zest*
> *Juice of 4 limes*
> 2 *egg whites*

1. Set the freezer control for fast freezing.
2. Remove the stems from the mint leaves and chop fine. In a saucepan, combine the mint leaves, water, and sugar. Bring to a boil, stirring until sugar dissolves. Cool.

3. Strain the cooled mixture. Add the corn syrup, lime zest, and juice.
   Freeze until firm.
4. Break up the mixture and beat to a smooth mush. Beat the egg whites
   until they stand in soft peaks. Fold into mixture and freeze until firm.

2 PINTS

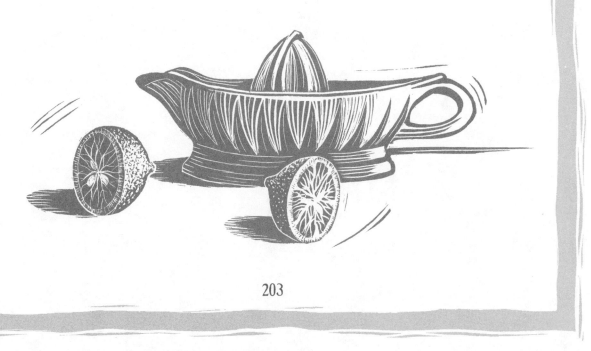

Fruit Bowl

A hearty or especially spicy dinner calls for a light hand with the dessert. Try this refreshing mixed fruit bowl with Lemon Thyme Cookies (page 168) or gingersnaps for a perfect ending. The fruits can be varied with the season, with little chance of putting in the "wrong" one.

1 pint raspberries, fresh or frozen
1 ripe honeydew melon, scooped into balls
1 ripe cantaloupe, scooped into balls
1 pint sliced peaches, fresh or frozen
1 sweet orange, cut into chunks
1 grapefruit, cut into chunks
1 pint halved strawberries, fresh or frozen
1 pint fresh blueberries, if available
2 tablespoons finely chopped fresh mint or 1 teaspoon dried
1 tablespoon finely chopped fresh lemon balm
Sugar to taste (start with ½ cup)
2 ounces Cointreau or other orange-based liqueur
1 banana, sliced
1 kiwifruit, sliced

1. Place the raspberries, melon balls, peaches, orange chunks, grapefruit chunks, strawberries, and blueberries in a large, decorative glass bowl. Gently toss with the mint, lemon balm, sugar, and liqueur. Refrigerate for an hour or more.
2. The citrus will keep the peaches from discoloring, but you'll still want to add the banana slices just before serving. Decorate with the black-seeded kiwifruit.

8–12 SERVINGS

Rosemary Pears

The delicacy of pears is enhanced by an almost candied taste and the fragrance of rosemary. The pears should be ripe but still firm so they will hold their shape in the cooking.

> 3 *ripe pears*
> *Zest of half a lemon*
> ½ *teaspoon finely chopped rosemary*
> 1½ *tablespoons sugar*
> 1 *tablespoon butter*
> ½ *cup dry white wine*
> 3 *tablespoons brandy*

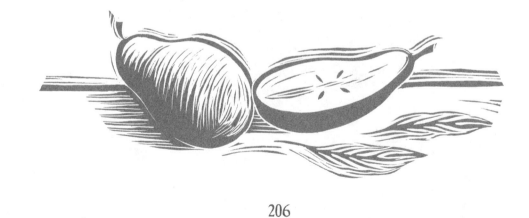

1. Preheat the oven to 300°F.
2. Cut the unpeeled pears lengthwise, removing the blossom and stem ends and scooping out the seeds with a melon baller. With foil, line a casserole that will hold the pears in a single layer.
3. Set the pears in the dish, skin side down. Sprinkle lemon zest, then rosemary and sugar over the pears, and dot with butter. Pour wine into the bottom of the casserole.
4. Bake until the pears are cooked but not soft, about 15 minutes, depending on the pears. Then place the pears under the broiler until the sugar turns slightly brown. Spoon the brandy into the seed cavities, light with a match, and let burn for about a minute.

6 SERVINGS

*In early times, rosemary was
an emblem of fidelity.*

Peach-Plum Chutney

The gold of peaches, yellow plums, mustard seed, and turmeric characterizes this tasty chutney, a tangy offset for the mild flavor of poached or baked fish or chicken.

CINNAMON BASIL WHITE WINE VINEGAR
> 2 tablespoons ground cinnamon
> 2 tablespoons white wine vinegar
> 2 cups basil leaves

1. Tie the cinnamon in a square of muslin or cheesecloth. Put the vinegar in a stainless steel saucepan and add the cinnamon. Heat the mixture to 110°F. Remove the pan from the heat and let the vinegar cool slightly. Pour into a container for steeping.
2. Remove the stems from the basil leaves and add the leaves to the vinegar. Cover the container tightly and set in a dark place at room temperature. Shake the container every few days. Check the flavor after a week. If the flavor is not strong enough, let it continue to set for up to a month.
3. Strain the vinegar, put it in a storage container, and seal tightly.

Peach-Plum Chutney

1½ pounds freestone peaches, pitted and chopped

1½ pounds yellow plums, pitted and chopped

1 cup chopped white onion

1 sweet yellow pepper, cored, seeded, and chopped

2 tablespoons fresh minced ginger

1 garlic clove, minced

1 fresh green or red hot pepper, seeded and minced

2 cups packed light brown sugar

1 cup cinnamon basil white wine vinegar

½ cup fresh cinnamon basil, minced

1 tablespoon fresh lemon zest

1 teaspoon mustard seeds

1 teaspoon ground cloves

1 teaspoon ground cinnamon

½ teaspoon ground coriander seeds

½ teaspoon turmeric

2 teaspoons non-iodized salt

1. Using a food processor, chop the fruits and vegetables. Combine all ingredients in an 8-quart heavy-bottomed pot. Bring to a boil, stirring constantly. Reduce the heat and simmer for 20 minutes, stirring often.

2. Pour into hot half-pint jars with two-piece canning lids and process by the boiling water bath method (jars on a rack, submerged in boiling water) for 15 minutes.

6 HALF-PINT JARS

Rhubarb Chutney

In springtime, when rhubarb sprouts its crisp red stalks, the simmering of this colorful and spicy chutney will send a delightful aroma through the house. Preserved, it can be enjoyed all year as a condiment with rice and meats.

1 *cup dried cherries*
7 *cups chopped rhubarb*
1 *cup red onion, chopped*
1½ *cups apple, cored and chopped*
3 *garlic cloves, minced*
1 *tablespoon minced fresh ginger*
½ *cup minced fresh lovage*
2 *cups packed light brown sugar*
1 *cup red wine vinegar*
1 *teaspoon each of ground cinnamon, cloves, allspice,*
and coriander seeds

1. Combine all ingredients in an 8-quart heavy-bottomed pot. Stirring constantly, heat until boiling.
2. Reduce heat and simmer about 30 minutes, stirring often. Pour into hot half-pint jars with two-piece canning lids and process by the boiling water bath method (jars on a rack, submerged in boiling water) for 15 minutes.

6 HALF-PINT JARS

Herb Crabapple Jelly

Herbs blend wonderfully with apples and crabapples. If you can find cooking crabapples (the ones from the decorative trees are not the same), the jelly will have a glorious rosy color. Apples have enough natural pectin to make jelly on their own.

> 2 cups apple juice
> ½ cup mint, basil thyme, lemon verbena,
>   rose geranium, or tarragon leaves
> ¾ cup granulated sugar

1. Combine ingredients in saucepan. Heat until sugar dissolves and mixture has jelled, about 30 minutes.
2. Pour into hot, sterilized canning jars with two-piece lids, leaving a ¼-inch headspace. Process 5 minutes in a boiling water bath (place jars on a rack in a deep kettle and cover with water until about ¼ inch over lids).

2 HALF-PINT JARS

Minted Wine Jelly

Muscatel, product of the muscat grape, is a sweet dessert wine with a gold or amber color. Add one of the mints and you'll have a flavorful replacement for the traditional apple mint jelly.

> 2 cups muscatel
> 3 cups sugar
> ½ bottle liquid fruit pectin
> 3 tablespoons chopped fresh mint leaves
> Sprigs of fresh mint

1. In the top of a double boiler, cook the wine and sugar over rapidly boiling water, stirring constantly. It will take about 2 minutes for the sugar to dissolve.
2. Remove top of double boiler from heat, stir in the pectin, and add the mint.
3. Place a sprig of mint in each sterilized, half-pint glass jar (with two-piece canning lids). Seal at once, and store in a cool place.

4 HALF-PINT JARS

Herb Jellies

Piquant jellies can be made with any number of fresh herbs: basil, lemon verbena, marjoram, mint, parsley, rosemary, sage, tarragon, or thyme. This basic recipe can be used for any one of them, or they can be combined. Rosemary and tarragon, for instance, live together nicely, as do basil and parsley. Sage and cilantro, on the other hand, would clash.

2½   cups boiling water
  1   cup fresh herbs, leaves and stems, plus 10 leaves for garnish
4½   cups granulated sugar
 ¼   cup lemon juice or vinegar
 ½   bottle liquid pectin

1. In a saucepan, pour the boiling water over the herbs, cover, and let stand for 20 minutes.
2. Add sugar and lemon juice to the infusion. Heat until sugar dissolves. Bring mixture to a boil and add pectin. Boil for 1 minute, stirring constantly.
3. Remove from heat and skim off the foam. Place a few fresh herb leaves into each jelly jar. Pour into jars with two-piece canning lids and process 5 minutes in a boiling hot water bath with jars submerged.

4 HALF-PINT JARS

If the day and the night are such
that you greet them with joy,
and life emits a fragrance like flowers
and sweet-scented herbs . . . that is your success.

—Henry David Thoreau

Tomato Herb Jelly

In September, when the garden is too full of tomatoes and the air is pretty clear of humidity, the time is right for making jams and jellies. This combination of tomatoes and herbs has a dash of hotness and will make an excellent condiment to serve with meat or chicken dishes. It will taste good on toast, as well.

¼ cup chopped fresh sage or crushed fresh marjoram
¼ cup crushed fresh thyme
1 cup water
1 cup tomato juice
Dash of Tabasco or other hot, red sauce
Juice of 3 lemons, strained (about ½ cup)
2 cups honey
2 cups granulated sugar
6 ounces liquid pectin

1. In a small saucepan, combine the herbs with the water. Simmer gently for 5 minutes. Remove from heat and let stand for 30 minutes.
2. In a large stainless-steel or enameled pot, combine the tomato juice, hot sauce, lemon juice, honey, and sugar. Strain the herbs. Add the herb water and 2 teaspoons of the cooked herbs to the tomato mixture. (Discard the remaining cooked herbs.) Bring to a rapid boil. Add the pectin and boil rapidly for 1 minute.
3. Remove from heat and skim off the foam. Fill hot, sterilized (boiled 5 minutes in water to cover) half-pint jars with two-piece lids with the tomato mixture, leaving a ¼-inch headspace. Seal and process for 5 minutes in a boiling water bath.

6–8 HALF-PINT JARS

Marjoram symbolizes joy and is associated with young love.

Rutabaga Marmalade

A rutabaga by any other name is a turnip: a large, yellow, edible tuber. It seems an unlikely candidate for a sweet preserve, but here it is.

> 2 pounds rutabaga, peeled and chopped (5 cups)
> 5 oranges, chopped with peels on
> Juice of 3 lemons
> 5 cups sugar
> 1 cup water
> 1 teaspoon finely chopped fresh thyme or ⅓
>   teaspoon dried

1. Simmer the rutabaga for 5 minutes until tender but still firm. Drain.
2. Combine with the oranges, lemon juice, sugar, water, and thyme. Cook over high heat, stirring frequently until syrup begins to jell. Overcooking will result in a mixture that is too thick.
3. Ladle into canning jars with two-piece lids, seal, and process in boiling water bath for 5 minutes.

5 HALF-PINT JARS

Thyme is symbolic of strength and courage.

Lemon Balm Lemonade

A little extra tang is brought to old-fashioned lemonade with the addition of lemon balm. For those who want the shortcut, make the herb infusion and add it to frozen concentrate.

> 4 lemons, scrubbed
> Small bunch of lemon balm (about 3 ounces)
> ½ cup sugar
> ⅔ cup boiling water
> 2½ cups water
> Extra lemon balm sprigs for garnishing

1. Peel off the rinds of the lemons, avoiding the white part. Put the rinds in a small bowl. Tear off the lemon balm leaves and add them to the rinds. Add the sugar. Pour in the boiling water and stir well, crushing the leaves to release their flavor. Let this mixture stand for about 15 minutes.
2. Cut the lemons in half and squeeze out the juice. Put a few fresh sprigs of lemon balm into a large glass pitcher, then strain the lemon juice into it and add the cooled, strained syrup. Add the rest of the water, or half water and half ice cubes, and chill.

1 QUART

Mint Juleps

The classic drink of the South, a mint julep evokes images of antebellum ladies on wide verandas and gentlemen paying them calls. In reality, it's a potent drink with a sweet, minty chill. For the best effect, put glasses in the freezer long enough to frost them.

Splash of soda water
3 sprigs of mint
1 teaspoon sugar
1½ ounces bourbon
1 paper-thin slice of lime

1. Combine the soda water, sugar, and 2 of the mint sprigs.
2. Pour the bourbon into a 10-ounce glass that has been filled with finely crushed ice.
3. Add the soda water, sugar, and mint mixture. Decorate with a sprig of mint and the slice of lime.

1 SERVING

Index

Converting Recipe Measurements to Metric

Use the following formulas for converting U.S. measurements to metric. Since the conversions are not exact, it's important to convert the measurements for all of the ingredients to maintain the same proportions as the original recipe.

WHEN THE MEASUREMENT GIVEN IS	MULTIPLY IT BY	TO CONVERT TO
teaspoons	4.93	milliliters
tablespoons	14.79	milliliters
fluid ounces	29.57	milliliters
cups (liquid)	236.59	milliliters
cups (liquid)	.236	liters
cups (dry)	275.31	milliliters
cups (dry)	.275	liters
pints (liquid)	473.18	milliliters
pints (liquid)	.473	liters
pints (dry)	550.61	milliliters
pints (dry)	.551	liters
quarts (liquid)	946.36	milliliters
quarts (liquid)	.946	liters
quarts (dry)	1101.22	milliliters
quarts (dry)	1.101	liters
gallons	3.785	liters
ounces	28.35	grams
pounds	.454	kilograms
inches	2.54	centimeters
degrees Fahrenheit (Centigrade)	$5/9$ (temperature − 32)	degrees Celsius

While standard metric measurements for dry ingredients are given as units of mass, U.S. measurements are given as units of volume. Therefore, the conversions listed above for dry ingredients are given in the metric equivalent of volume.